We Thought We had it Made

"I first met Alan Menzies in Randers, Denmark. He was playing drums with The Bootles, a Beatles cover band. We met in the office of CB and Ollie, a Danish agent whom we shared as both agent and friend.

Alan was not just the drummer of the band but also very much the tour manager. A proud Liverpool man with a penchant for colourful language (sorry, Alan, but it's true). He became my tour manager after a very successful CD I recorded in Denmark called 'Johnny Logan and Friends'.

Alan is one of those real characters that you are lucky enough to have walk through your life. A funny, intelligent and thoughtful man who could have you crying with laugher one moment and helping you with advice the next. He has so many real stories from his life on the road and the people he's worked with.

I wish my friend all the best with this book and I hope to meet up with him again down that road of music that is our life."

Johnny Logan (singer/songwriter/3 times Eurovision Song Contest Winner)

"It was a great pleasure for us to tour with Alan in Denmark and England. We love Alan. A great, talented guy who is also very funny."

Linda Gail Lewis (singer/musician and sister of Jerry Lee Lewis)

"The first time I heard Alan play was at Butlins in Ayr, Scotland, in 1990. He was playing in a three-piece band and I was very impressed with the sound they made for just three guys.

I saw him play a number of times over the years and in 2016 I invited him to play with my band, The Attraction. He has done so on a number of occasions since then.

Alan is a funny guy and easy to work with."

Vince Earl (singer/actor (Brookside))

We Thought We had it Made

Memoirs of drummer Alan Menzies
(you lucky people!)

Written by Linda M Barrett

First published 2020

Acknowledgements

A massive thank you to those who supplied photos and images and/or gave permission for them to be used.

Cover photo courtesy of Billy Gill

Every effort has been made to trace copyright holders of all images and where possible they have been credited except where they have requested not to be.

We would also like to thank the following for their contributions to this book.
The National Archives
Rob Nisbet
Annette White
Susan Foulkes

Formatting by Rebecca Emin

In Memory of

We would like to remember everyone mentioned in this book who is no longer with us, in particular:

John Turner Menzies, Jessie Dorothy Menzies (Dol), Calle Nielson, Ronnie Malpas
Mike McKay, Wally Halsall, John White, John McCaffrey, Agnes Muir (nee Croft)
Torben Dahl (Benny), Cliff Wilks, Tommy Jenson, Brent Pickthall

Contents

Introduction

I was 16 when I first met Alan Menzies, in January 1965. He played drums in a group called Rhythm and Blues Incorporated and I worked behind the coffee bar at my local Palais, where they regularly played.

Their debut single, Louie Louie, had been released earlier in the month and they were going to appear on the trendy TV show, Ready Steady Go, at the end of it.

A lot of top groups and singers played Bolton Palais in those days; people who were topping the charts. I remember Lulu and Procol Harum playing there but there were many others. Rhythm and Blues Incorporated were always my favourite. They easily held their own amongst the big names and always filled the place. And it rocked! Later that year, when their fan club secretary, Aggie Croft, had to give up the role I took it over.

At about the time that I took over the fan club Alan left Rhythm and Blues Incorporated. It was July 1965 and he was just 17. He left with the idea of heading down to London, with fellow band member, lead guitarist, Barry Womersley, to find fame and fortune.

I lost contact with him for many years. We got back in touch, through Facebook, in 2013. These days I count him amongst my closest friends.

Over the last three years we have spent many, many hours together, and apart, sitting at computers or recording on Dictaphones with numerous e-mails, messages, texts and phone calls ricocheting back and forth.

As much as possible I have tried to stay true to Alan's own voice in the telling of his story.

Ready, Steady, Go: Show #78 -- 29-Jan-65

--The Animals
--TheHollies
--The Who
--Donovan
--Ron and Mel
--Elkie Brooks
--Goldie and the Gingerbreads
--Rick and Sandy
--Rhythm and Blues, Inc

Ready! Steady! Go!

It was on a freezing cold January morning when our road manager, Wally Halsall, dropped us off at a small airfield in Southport, Lancashire; Pete Kelly, Barry Womersley, Mike McKay, John McCaffrey and me; collectively known as Rhythm and Blues Incorporated.

Christmas was over, and a brand-new year had just begun. It was 1965 and we were certain, beyond all doubt, that it would be ours. We'd recently cut our first record, Louie Louie, and we were on our way to London for our debut TV appearance to promote it.

There was a photographer, from The Southport Visiter, waiting for us when we arrived, and we posed for a few pictures before we climbed aboard the Gregory Air Taxi and took to the air for the next step of our exciting, new career.

There were two programs back in the '60s which were guaranteed to have teenagers glued to their TV sets. *Top of the Pops* was broadcast on BBC, on Thursday evenings, and *Ready Steady Go (RSG)* went out on ITV (then ATV), on Friday nights.

It was hosted by Keith Fordyce and Cathy McGowan. Like Top of the Pops it featured the most popular groups and singers of the day. It always opened with the line *The Weekend Starts Here!*

We found out we were going to be on the show in November '64. We used to play at the college balls at Oxford University and on this particular night our manager, Jim Turner, pitched up. We were there with the writer, Thom Keyes. If I remember rightly he was on the Entertainment Committee. I'd been chatting to him quite a bit and he was intrigued by some of the Liverpool slang I used. In fact, he subsequently wrote a book called *All Night Stand* and I believe he included some of the words and phrases that he learned from me that night. 'Last' (meaning horrible) seemed to be his favourite.

We were in the library, I think, when Jim told us. He simply said, 'I've got you on Ready Steady Go in January,' like it was the most normal thing in the world. We were stunned.

Rhythm and Blues Incorporated was my first recording group and we'd recorded Louie Louie, that September. It was going to be released in early January '65. We were scheduled, it seemed, to appear on the programme at the end of January. To say we were ecstatic would be a colossal understatement. At 17 I was the youngest member of the band, but we were all just kids really. We were still trying to get our heads round having made a record and now we were being told that we were about to appear on one of the most popular TV programmes of the day.

But, the best laid plans and all that; as usual there was a problem. RSG was filmed live, in London, at 6:30, on Fridays and we were booked to play at the Floral Hall, in Southport, that night. We couldn't get out of it so it was something of a predicament. In the end our manager had to pay for us to fly from Woodvale Airfield, in Southport, to a small airfield in London (I can't remember the name of it). It was the only way we could manage to do both gigs.

None of us had ever flown before. It was amazing! I remember Barry, our lead guitarist, saying nervously, 'Whoever sits in the front don't touch anything! Seriously, don't touch anything!' In the end it was him who sat there so he was fine.

After we'd landed in London we were taken, by limo, to the studio. We were met by Cathy McGowan who told us how much she liked our record and she took us to where it was all filmed.

I'm not quite sure what I'd expected but the level of chaos there, that day, wasn't it. Not much seemed to go according to plan. I remember at rehearsals, every time they wanted Hilton Valentine, they couldn't find him anywhere. The producers were going ballistic. Then one of them yelled, in the most upper-class voice I'd ever heard, 'Who is this man? Take his name!' I thought he was going to explode and I couldn't get over the fact that he didn't even know his name.

Then The Hollies' drums weren't on stage, when they should've been, and they couldn't find any of the band. The Animals had just done their bit and their kit was still there so that also caused a lot of panic. It did all come together in the end though I never worked out how.

I used Keith Moon's drums for the session but we weren't allowed to play live because we were the new guys. We had to mime to the record. Only The Animals and The Hollies were allowed to play live. And Donovan, as he was just a one-man band with a guitar. The rest of us had to mime.

Finally, they let the kids in and it was all stations go. I remember the crew shouting for The Hollies and

Graham Nash running in cursing because they'd been playing cards, in the dressing room, and he'd been winning.

We went on about third or fourth. They'd just put 'Rhythm and Blues' on the sign. Jim remonstrated with them but they hadn't left enough room for 'Incorporated' so someone came down and just stuck 'Inc' underneath.

To our immense relief we went down really well and the kids seemed to love us. Unfortunately, we had to leave straight after doing our bit to get back to Southport for our gig there.

The driver was about half an hour late picking us up and a very agitated Jim Turner had a real go at him when he finally arrived. To be fair it turned out not to be his fault. Winston Churchill's funeral was the next day and there'd been a rehearsal for it. Half of London had been cordoned off. We had a hell of a job getting to the airfield and a very anxious looking pilot was standing by the plane looking out for us when we arrived. We were bundled into the aircraft and before we knew it we were in the air on our way back to Southport.

The 29th January 1965 was, in fact, a massive day for me on two counts. Not only was it my first national TV appearance, but it was also the day I got my Ludwig drum kit.

Because I was in London, our roadie, Wally, went into Liverpool with my dad to get it. My dad had to go with him to sign because I was buying it on hire purchase and we were both underage. The drums cost £288 which was a fortune in the mid '60s. I'd had a Premier kit up to then, but the Ludwig was the crème de la crème of drums.

The trouble was that I couldn't actually afford the whole kit. Now Clive Hornby was the drummer in The Dennisons before he went into acting and became Jack Sugden in Emmerdale. One night he'd set up his Ludwig kit in the dressing room of the Locarno in Liverpool.

They were stunning, and I said to him, 'I'd love to have some, but I can't afford them.'

He said to me 'Buy the kit without the snare drum and cymbals and use the ones from your old Premier kit. It'll make it cheaper.' And that's what I did.

My Premier kit had some history as it goes. It had once belonged to Ringo Starr briefly. Apparently, he hadn't liked the plastic heads on it. They were just coming in, but he preferred pig or calf skin. He'd bought the kit from Frank Hessy's in Stanley Street, Liverpool and he'd only had them a couple of weeks when he took them back so Hessy's exchanged them and I ended up with the original plastic headed kit.

I played my new Ludwig kit, for the first time, at the Floral Hall that night. And I am still playing them to this day.

As we approached Woodvale Airfield we saw naked flames marking out the runway. We thought it was the coolest thing we'd ever seen. Wally was waiting for us. He was flashing the headlights and revving up the van engine before we'd even got off the plane.

'Come on, Guys!' he yelled. 'There are eleven hundred plus people waiting to hear you play!'

At last we got to the venue and it was absolutely

chokka. I seem to remember there were 1,157 people there. I'm told that to this day we still hold the record for the largest number of people in the Floral Hall.

RSG was broadcast live at 6:30 in the south but in the north, it wasn't on till 10:30. When we got to The Floral Hall they'd put huge TVs on either side of the stage. And they'd made sure that the word was out that they had them and that people didn't have to stay in to watch the programme. Clever!

They asked us not to do Louie Louie in the first set, so we didn't. We came off and at 10:30 they put the TVs on for RSG. After the program, we went back on stage and did Louie Louie. The place erupted. It was mind blowing.

We really thought we had it made!

Rhythm and Blues Incorporated just before they boarded the plane, at Woodvale, to take them to London.
From left to right: Mike McKay, John McCaffrey, Alan Menzies, Pete (now Kin) Kelly and Barry Womersley.

Courtesy of The Southport Visiter

The Early Years

Mine was a very typical 1950s working class upbringing, I think. I was born on 5th August 1947 in Mill Rd Hospital, in Liverpool. My father worked on the docks and my mother was a housewife.

My earliest memory is of us sharing a house with my grandma, Auntie Alice and Uncle Ernie at 41 Thirlemere Rd in Anfield; and it was a really small house let me tell you. It was pretty cramped.

Then, in 1951, my parents were able to buy a small house of their own. So, the three of us moved to 26 Sapphire St, in the Old Swan area of Liverpool.

It was a two up, two down, terraced house just like the ones you see on Coronation St. A lot of people my age will know the type, the front door led into a little porch, which people called a vestibule, and this led straight into the living room. There was a back kitchen from where the stairs led up to two bedrooms. There was no bathroom and the toilet was at the bottom of the yard. On Sunday afternoons a tin bath would be put in front of the fire and we took it in turns to have our baths. I generally got it last. I expect a lot of people will remember that.

They will probably also remember the Coronation. I was 5 when Queen Elizabeth was crowned, on 2nd June 1953, and we, like thousands of other people all over the country, had a street party. My mother had not long before bought me a sailor suit. Because of this the organisers of our party asked her if I could be the Duke of Edinburgh. Of course, she said yes! They had a draw to choose the Queen and the girl who won it was a girl, my age, called Joan McNamara; everybody called her Joan Mac. I remember they wanted us to walk up the street holding hands and we both flatly refused! Yes, it is possible to be mortified at the age of 5.

The residents had saved up for this party for ages. I remember a woman, called Nelly Quinn, coming to the house, every Sunday, to collect 6d (6 old pennies). Then on the day of the Coronation a bus came, from Liverpool Corporation, to take all the kids for a drive around Liverpool. The adults had to rush out and stop it coming up the street because it nearly brought all the decorations down.

Then in the afternoon we had the street party. There was a bombed area at the top of our street and we had the party there. Me and Joan Mac had to sit at the top of the table. Then, it seems, there was some money left over and so we had another do the following Saturday.

The Making of a Drummer

I went to St Mary's Primary School and it was from there, when I was 8, that I joined The Cubs. There was a church parade on the first Sunday of every month and we marched from the school hall, where we met, to St Mary's church, about half a mile away.

The Boys' Brigade used to practise in that church hall and if we were a bit early we would see them come out and march down to the church. I loved it when we did, and I would watch them in awe, especially the drummers. I thought, *Great band!* I think I was a bit star-struck really. I used to memorise the tune that they played and when I got home I'd get a couple of sticks and tap out the beat on the kitchen table. I genuinely thought that anyone could do it. My love of drums was born.

Then someone in the Scouts decided it would be a good idea for them to have a band. We Cubs used to meet in the school hall on Friday evenings, from 6:30 to 7:45, and, after we'd finished, the Scouts had their band practice there. One night we went in their room to get our coats, and their drums were there. I shouldn't really have done it, but I picked up the sticks and just started drumming, I actually played, what I now know to be two 3s and a 7. I couldn't understand why everyone was staring at me in surprise.

On another night, I was probably around 10 by this time, I started messing around on their drums and there was a guy, called Albert Pye, there with a couple of his other musician mates. One of them was called Ronnie Price. I can't remember the other one's name. Albert was in the Boys' Brigade and he was teaching our scout troop to play the drums. They were all in their late teens, I would think, a lot older than me, anyway. When I started playing the drums Albert just turned around and smiled. He asked me to play it again, so I did and then he asked if I could stay after everyone had gone. He asked me to play certain things then he asked me to play this particular tune.

Ronnie Price nodded towards the third guy, they were with, and said, 'He's been trying to play that for weeks!'

The Cubs' night was later changed to Wednesdays, but the Scouts kept to Fridays so that put an end to that. I always thought it was lucky that I was there before the change though or I would never have had the chance to play when I did and probably would never have met Ronnie Price.

When I was 11 I went into The Scouts. There wasn't a drum available for me, but I always used to hang around at band practice and one day the scout master asked me if I could handle a snare drum as one of their regular drummers was sick. I was only little but assured him I could. He let me take one home and clever me goes and adjusts the strap for the length. This cleverness resulted in a huge bruise on my leg because I'd set it too low. That was a lesson well learned.

The fact that I'd been given a drum caused a lot of problems with some parents whose sons had been in the troop for a long time. I was actually there when one mum and dad complained to the Scout Leader. They were upset that I'd only been in the troop 5 minutes and had a drum.

I remember him saying to them, 'Please don't make me do this. Don't make me humiliate your son. But if you insist, bring him down; we'll try him out and see who the best player is. I need a drummer for Sunday. Your son would need training. Alan doesn't.'

I don't think they were very happy, but they went away and I kept the drum.

The Scouts had dances on Friday nights and there was always a dance band playing. One night, one of the lads went up and got me a go on the drums. Everyone stood around listening. I was really nervous, but I must have done okay because I got a round of applause at the end. It was the first proper drum kit I'd ever played. The feeling of the bounce from the drums when I hit them, that first time, was exhilarating. It was a feeling I'll never forget.

Then Ronnie Price set up a band with himself as the lead singer. Again, I can't remember the name of it. He needed a drummer and he'd heard I'd got a small set of drums. I'd got them from somebody's brother-in-law at school for about £3.

The guitarists were Les Heinz (Bean), Kenny Corns and Gordon Kenny. We played a few times for the Scouts and Girl Guides and then we started to get proper gigs. The trouble was that as I was only around 12 I couldn't do them because they were on licensed premises. In those days you weren't even allowed on the premises if you weren't 18. In the end they had to do them without me. I was gutted.

I remember another occasion when I was in a group called The Kestrels with a couple of school friends, Jimmy Whitefield and Ronnie Davis and we got a gig in this club. Most of us were underage but they could pass for 18. I was 13 but looked 10. They had to hide me in the snooker room till it was time to play.

In 1961 we moved to Southport. My father was a boiler maker on the railways by this time. Of course, it was all steam engines then. He said he left the docks because he was fed up of going on strike. It was less money on the railways but it was regular. He worked 7 days a week and they used to call him out, at all hours, for breakdowns and stuff, but he still preferred it.

I left The Scouts when we moved and obviously changed schools. We moved in the July and I thought I wouldn't have to start till September, but my dad had other ideas: 'There's two weeks left yet,' he said, 'and you'll go.' And that was that. I had to go for those last two weeks of the year. I then went into the final year that September. I used to go back to Liverpool at the weekends for a while but that eventually fizzled out.

I was 14 by now and some of the lads in my class used to go to the YMCA on Friday nights. They had groups on there and the first one I ever saw there was called The Teenbeats. They were awesome. I'd never heard or seen anything like it.

One day, John Wilkinson, the drummer, (who I'm still in contact with, even though he now lives in America) broke the head on one of his tom toms.

So, I said to him, 'I'll swap the heads for you if you want. Save you turning it upside down.'

He agreed, and I did it. He was really made up and gave me half a crown (2/6 shillings = approximately 15p but it was worth a lot more in those days).

Then one night I actually got up and played for them. John Wilkie was made up. I played guitar for them once, too, at the Glen Park Club, in Southport. I played Apache. It was the only thing I knew, haha. I went around with them for a few months. They even gave me a group jumper. Amazing! It opened a door to a brand-new world for me.

Alan, aged 5, in his sailor suit. Courtesy of Alan Menzies

Alan in The Scouts
Courtesy of Alan Menzies

The Early Band

I was still 14 when one night I went to Meols Cop Youth Club; I practise there now, funnily enough. There was a group on, called Yan and the Vendettas, and, for some reason, their drummer didn't want to be there so I got up and played with them. He just went home and I joined them that night. I didn't even know what a vendetta was. I remember our next-door neighbour saying to me, 'Do you know what a vendetta is?' I didn't! But it was my first *proper* band.

I stopped going around with The Teenbeats then but when I had followed them their manager had been a guy called Mike Birchall. For some reason they'd gone their separate ways and Mike had opened an agency. He started getting involved with a band called Chris and the Quiet Ones who were from Formby. Their drummer was a guy called Barry Madden but again he wanted to leave.

I was coming up for 15 now and I'd got myself a proper drum kit. The first bass drum I ever got was a Stratford. It cost me £12 and I paid half a crown a week for it.

Anyway, Mike Birchall contacted me and asked if I wanted to join this group. He was changing the name to The Gems. I left Yan and the Vendettas then and joined them.

The first gig we ever did was at The Guild Hall, in Formby. I got the S2 bus from Duke St in Southport to get to it. Formby was just a sleepy, little village back then.

The line-up was George Eccles (lead guitar), John White (bass guitar), Ray O'Connell (rhythm guitar),

Chris Rimmer (lead singer) and myself on drums. Chris Rimmer left about 5 or 6 weeks after I joined them, and Dai Davis became lead vocals.

I remember us doing a gig at SS Empire in York. We got £13 which we thought was a fortune. We normally earned £5-7. Funny when you think how far we travelled for that.

George then left the group some months later and we got a guy called John Murphy to play lead guitar. He eventually went on to play for a group, called The Four Just Men, who had quite a lot of success around Liverpool and beyond.

In early 1963 Rhythm and Blues Incorporated started up. I knew Mick Tocker who, at the time, was their road manager. He was running them around in a hired van. He actually used to run us (The Gems) around in his Bedford van. George Eccles was playing with them by then. I also knew the lead singer, Pete Kelly, and the bass guitarist, John McCaffrey, just from the circuit really. The rhythm guitarist was a guy called Mick Foden. He nearly blew his finger off when he plugged his guitar straight into the wall one night. He was lucky he didn't kill himself. He left after that and they got Mike McKay. At the time the drummer was a guy called Barry Tweedale. I don't know what happened to him but suddenly he was gone, and I was asked to join.

Of course, I was still with The Gems but at about this time John White was leaving. This meant we had no bass player. The guys in the band were going to carry on without one.

I said, 'You can't carry on without a bass player,' but we ended up doing this gig in Manchester without one. It didn't work for me. I left at that point and joined Rhythm and Blues Incorporated.

Alan aged 14
Courtesy of Alan Menzies

Rhythm and Blues Incorporated

When I first joined R & B Inc the line-up was Pete (now Kin) Kelly (lead vocal), George Eccles (lead guitar), John McCaffrey ((Mac) bass guitar), Mike McKay (rhythm guitar) and me on drums.

Though I consider it to be my first serious recording group we all still had jobs as well, at the start. Pete Kelly was a telegraph boy, John was a window dresser at Broadbent's Department Store. I worked there too, in the dispatch Department. George worked at Johnson's the dry cleaners as a machine operator and Mike McKay worked for the Inland Revenue, in Liverpool. I was earning the grand sum of £3 17s 6d at Broadbent's. Juggling the two did not always make for an easy life.

I remember once having a day off work because we'd entered a competition at the Philharmonic Hall, in Liverpool. It was a beat competition for Liverpool bands. I'd worked extra hours beforehand so that I could have this time off. It was on a Wednesday as I recall. We went there, did our bit, and then we had to go back later in the day to get the results.

While we waited we went to The Cavern for lunch. We'd just got there when Ronnie Malpass, who was our manager at the time, said, 'I've left all my bullshit in the car. I'll have to go and get it.' So, off he went, and we carried on into The Cavern.

The owner of the club was a guy called Ray McFall and the DJ was Bob Wooler. Bob had a lot of say in what went on in The Cavern though and he booked all the bands. He actually introduced The Beatles to Brian Epstein.

Anyway, we went into The Cavern and we got talking to Bob Wooler. He offered us three gigs at £5 a gig. Not bad money in those days. We were ready to snap it up but Ronnie Malpass came back and he wasn't having any of it. He argued with him over the fee and, in the end, we just got the one gig for £6. I can remember Pete Kelly going ballistic and calling Ronnie a complete clown. Ronnie insisted we would be better thought of but that was absolute nonsense; we weren't. In fact, we never played there again. It's in the Cavern's book though that we played that one night. And we are on The Cavern Wall of Fame. Not many can say that.

So, after we left The Cavern that day, we went back to the Philharmonic Hall, to get the results of the competition. Ronnie Malpass goes in first and he comes running out. 'We've made it through, lads,' he says. 'We're coming back tomorrow for the next round.' We were all elated. Mac and I decided that we just wouldn't go in to work the next day. We all arranged to meet at 9am, at Ronnie's club, The Mocambo, as we had to be back in Liverpool for 10:30.

The next morning, we meet up as planned and we were all there except Mac. I can't remember who it was now but someone we knew walked past and asked what we were up to.

'We're just waiting for Mac,' we told him.

'You'll have a bloody long wait,' he said. 'I've just seen him working in Broadbent's window.'

We were furious but for some reason we carried on waiting and he actually did turn up about half an hour later.

'Where the fuck have you been?' I said to him. I couldn't believe the reply.

'Well, I had a row with my mum this morning over not going into work and I ended up going in.'

Pete Kelly was livid because he realised that this could cost me my job. He gave Mac a real dressing down.

Anyway, we finally got to Liverpool only to be told that more bands had been eliminated and sadly we were one of them. We weren't even on after all that. Not a great day.

I went into work next day and all hell broke loose. My immediate manager was really angry. The departmental manager, Harold Taylor, made a really big deal of it. You'd have thought I'd murdered somebody.

The foreman said to me, 'You might get the sack for this, you know.'

But the woman in charge of personnel, Miss Emersley, was a really lovely lady. I was summoned to her office and she said to me, 'Look, Alan, you're going to have to decide if you want to be a full-time drummer or work here.'

I told her I'd work there and for a while that's how it was. Some months later, however, we all gave up our jobs and went professional.

We used to get some really good gigs. I remember one back in '63 when we played at The Marine Club in Southport with Gene Vincent and a few other bands, including The Outlaws, whose guitarists included Richie Blackmore and Chas Hodges, who later became one half of Chas and Dave. I remember the dynamo had gone on their van and they couldn't drive it so Ronnie Malpass drove them to Leigh Casino where they were also playing. He then brought them back to his house and they stayed the night there. We thought they must have been loaded but thinking back they probably weren't because it was long before Chas and Dave and Deep Purple and at the time they were just jobbing musicians like us.

Ronnie had a coffee bar beneath his club and the day after this gig The Outlaws were in there most of the day while their van was getting fixed. I used to wait on for Ronnie sometimes and I was working that day. Consequently, I got to know the group quite well. Nice guys. We just chatted all day.

Working in the coffee bar was always fun. They did meals during the day, but we didn't do fish and chips even though it was on the menu. There was, however, a fish and chip shop next door and If anybody ordered them I used to have to go around the back, to the chippy, and fetch them in.

In early '64 we played at one of The Beatles' parties. They'd had a gig at the Odeon, in Southport, with Gerry and The Pacemakers. Ronnie Appleby, who ran beat nights at The Marine Club knew them well and he threw a party for them there. And he asked us to play! My God! We were ecstatic. Paul McCartney sat at the front and watched us. We were really made up if more than a little nervous. Even John Lennon chatted to us. He told us how he'd messed up his guitar, mainly with a screwdriver, trying to get the Bo Didley jungle sound out of it. He ended up having to cover it in black leather cloth and paint it. It was great to talk to him coz believe me, if Lennon didn't want to talk to you he wouldn't. He'd just turn his head and ignore you.

After that Ronnie Malpas got us in with the Alan Arnison Agency. They were one of the original agents in Manchester. We were with a guy called Ian Hamilton, who became very big in later years. He'd started out, in 1960, as a disc jockey at The Cresta Ballroom in Manchester and he also had the job of introducing the groups to the audience. He realised that many of them didn't have managers or agents, so he signed up half a dozen or so and joined them with the Alan Arnison Agency. Ian would get us the work. He would take 10%; and Ronnie would take 10%; it was all good fun, haha.

Ronnie bought us an old van to get to gigs in. He bought it from Latimers, in Shakespeare St, Southport, for £5 but he charged us £15. We didn't find out till later that he'd got it for a fiver.

They'd stopped using the van because it had no second gear. You had to go from first to third. None of us could drive, back then, but George had a provisional license, so we used to take this girl, Lynn, with us who could drive. Mind you to be honest she used to mainly sit in the back on Pete's knee. So, George did the driving until Mike got a license and then they shared it. I remember Ronnie Malpass teaching us all to drive and we all used to have a go at driving this van. He was a great guy in many ways to be fair.

We had a very good friend called Cliff Wilkes and he also taught me to drive. Cliff loved to come to our gigs and he'd help Wally with the driving. He worked so he couldn't come during the week. But he would almost always come with us at the weekends.

Sometimes we didn't get back until the Monday morning, but he had some arrangement with work that he could make the time up. Other times he took holiday to come with us. He would always go on about how much he loved it and we ended up nicknaming him Weekend. The lads would often say, 'Is Weekend coming this weekend?'

George eventually left the band and Barry Womersley came in as lead guitarist. We were getting very popular by now and had a really good following. Then we got in with a guy called Doug Martin. Brilliant guy! He worked for an agency in Waterloo, Liverpool, called Stewart Enterprises, on Stewart Rd.

He got us playing with Brian Kelly, at Beekay Promotions. Brian Kelly had booked The Beatles back in '61. He had seen the potential in them way back then. The girls were going mad for those guys even that far back.

He used to put on gigs at the Litherland Town Hall. In the early days he ran the Aintree Institute and he also put gigs on at The Lathom Hall in Seaforth but by the time we started playing with him he only had the Litherland Town Hall.

We backed Sonny Boy Williamson, at the Litherland, one Thursday night and the following Saturday at La Scala Ballroom, Runcorn because the band, I'm pretty sure it was The Yardbirds, who normally backed him couldn't do those nights.

When Brian gave us 10 bookings we couldn't believe it because we knew that the only other group he'd given ten bookings to had been The Beatles.

Brian Kelly also had his own sound company

called Alpha Sound, hiring PAs and other equipment to bands. We were starting to get a lot of work and going from strength to strength. We used to go around to his house on a Thursday night and one night this guy called Jim Turner arrived at his house. Brian Kelly had obviously told him about us and Jim said he wanted to manage us. He was telling us all what he could do for the band and, in the end, we went with him.

True to his word he got us a recording contract with Fontana and a spot on Ready Steady Go. He also got us a lot of work.

He was involved with the record companies to some extent and, as I said, he got us the record deal with Fontana. It belonged to Phillips actually, in Stanhope Place by Marble Arch. It's still there I think.

So, we went down there. We'd travelled down to London the night before because in those days the motorway only went as far as Stafford and then the M1 started again a lot further on, Watford Gap maybe. We stayed overnight at a place near Euston Station. It was a filthy, dirty place. The beds were crab-ridden. I remember saying to Mike, 'Don't get in that bed, Mike, it's full of crabs.'

So, he stuck his pyjama bottoms into his socks. But I think we all caught them. We called the place Crab Palace from then on. Needless to say, we never went back. The true side of rock 'n roll, eh!

The next day we went to the studio. Peter Lee Stirling (also known as Daniel Boone) was the producer. He had a big hit with 'Beautiful Sunday' which he co-wrote. We played 6 songs, including *Louie Louie* and the B side *Honey Don't*. I can remember, after we'd finished, Peter Lee Stirling turning to the engineer and saying, 'They're good. Very good.' We were made up.

Out of the 6 songs Peter Lee Stirling chose 'Louie Louie' and 'Honey Don't' to be recorded. We had to do 'Honey Don't' a couple of times because I kept slowing down. I don't know why; it was very unusual for me.

The record was released in the January of 1965. We were so excited and so confident it would be a hit. What we didn't bank on was that The Kinks would bring it out as well. There was no way we could compete with them.

As you might imagine our version of Louie Louie was number 1 in the Southport charts for weeks and weeks but only got to 38 in the National Top 40. I think The Kinks' version might have done better but we were essentially unknowns. You can still hear both numbers on YouTube though, to this day.

After RSG things just more or less went back to normal. It was a bit of a let-down, to be honest, after all the excitement of the record and the TV appearance. The night after RSG I remember we played at The La Scala Ballroom in Runcorn. It was a great gig and lots of people there but you couldn't help but feel it was a bit of an anti-climax. We then just carried on doing all the usual gigs. Nothing had changed except we had a record out.

There were highlights mind. We were once just chilling in Thom Keyes' mother's house when the phone rang. It was Jim Turner. Wayne Fontana was booked to do a gig at the Wednesbury Youth Club but for some reason he couldn't do it. Would we do it? I don't know how he found us. There were no mobile phones in those days but he'd somehow managed to track us down.

So off we went and rushed down to Wednesbury. It was a great youth club and we'd already played there four or five times before. The guy, Laurie, who ran it, was a really lovely, genuine bloke. My first crush was down there, a gorgeous girl, called Pam Peach. Far too nice for me! I'd met her when we'd played at the youth club, but it was pretty much unrequited love.

When we arrived, the carpark was heaving. Of course, people had gone there to see Wayne Fontana and we were quite worried they might be a bit anti to be lumbered with us. To our immense relief we learned that they had in fact been told what was going on and thankfully had chosen to stay. This was probably just after Louie Louie and RSG and we were still riding high. It turned out to be a really great gig for everyone.

We also did another huge gig at The Cambridge Hall in Southport for Ronnie Fern, now Lord Fern, but by and large everything just went back to normal. We did have a bit more money but that was about it.

We never got another record deal. I don't know why but, unfortunately, none of it had really led anywhere long term. We were told much later that there had been London agents and record producers who'd wanted us, including Mickie Most, but we didn't know that at the time and it would be hard to verify now. We were told that our management had, again, asked for too much money. It was a shame really because, even if I say so myself, we were a great band; we had the image; we were young and fresh, but we were inexperienced and very, very naive.

I became extremely disillusioned and Barry kept saying to me, 'Why don't we go down to London and see if we can make it there?'

By this time, I was heavily involved with my girlfriend, Irene, who eventually became my first wife, but luckily, she agreed to come down with us. So, we told the rest of the guys in the band we were leaving, and we played our last gig with Rhythm and Blues Incorporated at St Anne's Cricket Club in the July of 1965.

From left to right: Mike McKay, John McCaffrey,
Alan Menzies, George Eccles, Pete Kelly.
Courtesy of Kin Kelly

RHYTHM & BLUES INCORPORATED

Top left to right: Pete Kelly, John McCaffrey
Bottom left to right: Alan Menzies, Barry Womersley,
Mike McKay
Courtesy of Kin Kelly

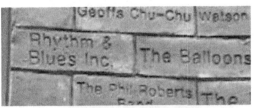

The Cavern Wall of Fame
Courtesy of Alan Menzies

After Rhythm and Blues Incorporated

Barry and I, of course, never did get to London. When I think about it now, my older self, we were extremely naïve. We didn't even have anywhere to go. We were just a couple of kids with big ideas that realistically could never have materialised; at least not then. Also, I was courting heavily with Irene at the time and I would have had her to support as well. She'd actually had every intention of coming with me and even gave up her job to do it. A really good job as well and then we didn't go. Her dad went absolutely ballistic.

I remember that the night after leaving Rhythm and Blues Incorporated Barry and I, along with Brent Pickthall and George Eccles played a gig at The Flying Dutchman, in Southport. After that I just started playing around, locally, doing different gigs with different bands and over the next three years I had a succession of bands and jobs.

My first job was in a garage, in Liverpool; then one day one of our regular customers, who was a builder, asked me how much money I was earning. I told him, and he offered me a job involving quite a substantial pay rise. So, I briefly became a builder. Very briefly. I'd only worked for him for about 10 days when I got a phone call from Blackpool from a member of Bruce and the Spiders. Their drummer had left to join The Rockin' Vickers and they offered me his job.

We played every night in Blackpool, so I went to live there. Irene had got another job by this time, albeit for less money, so we decided not to incur her father's wrath again and she stayed put.

One of the gigs was at a venue called The Foxhall which was very famous and popular. They still have live bands there to this day I think.

It was a really fun time but I only stayed a couple of months. I didn't really like being away from home. Then, The Rockin' Vickers split so I asked if the drummer might like his job back, which he did. I later found out that he'd actually been in touch with Dave Rossall, the front man, and fair play to Dave he'd told him that no way was he going to sack me. So, it was a good result for both of us in the end.

About six years later he got in touch to see if I'd be interested in emigrating to Australia with the Rossall family. I don't really know what their idea was because none of the other band members went. Maybe he was trying to take a ready-made band.

I'm now in contact with the other guitarist, Stuart, and he told me that Dave had eventually drunk himself to death. It really saddened me.

After I came home a local trumpet player, Dave Ederly, who played in a group called The Tabs contacted me and asked if I could do Sundays with his band as their drummer didn't want to do them. Within 3 months I was doing virtually all the gigs. The band was made up of a bunch of guys from Liverpool and Southport.

Again, I really enjoyed my time with them but, in the end, I left because I'd started doing private hire taxis, at the weekends. I couldn't do both and the taxis was where the money was. I could earn much more money doing that than playing drums and we needed the money.

I was juggling a few jobs around at that time. I've always been good at fixing cars and worked in a garage for a while as well as Alty's brickworks in Southport. I worked in their joinery department, building greenhouses. This would have been about November 1965.

It was also about then that I had my first car crash in my 1948 Morris Series E, which was the forerunner of the Morris Minor. It was pissing down with rain. I'd just picked up some petrol and was driving from Hesketh Bank to my home in Southport. It was a dark, miserable night and I had to drive past a corn mill in Tarleton.

They say you can never remember what happens just before an accident and that was certainly true for me. I can remember leaving the petrol station. The next thing this huge wagon was looming in front of me. It was backing into the corn factory. They used to do this all the time. I slammed the brakes on but it was too late. Luckily for me I hit him bang on the wheel; I could have gone under it and got crushed. Of course, there were no seat belts in those days. My face hit the steering wheel and I lost my two front teeth. One of them came out there and then. The other was a bit loose so I stupidly pulled it out. The dentist told me later that if I'd pushed it back in it probably would have tightened up. My mouth was a total mess but it could have been a lot worse. It really scared me.

No one, including me, even thought of going to the hospital. The police weren't really that interested either. They just took me to a mate's house nearby and he took me home. I rang Irene and she came over from Liverpool.

Now Irene lived in Oxenholme Crescent which was in the Norris Green area of the city. Her mother, Dot, who I liked to banter with, always told everyone they lived in West Derby because it was a bit posher. I used to joke with her about it all the time. We never did agree on where the boundary was. Nice lady. I liked her a lot.

It wasn't long after this that we found out that Irene was pregnant. We told her mother, who wasn't best pleased, and she suggested that she should tell Irene's dad, rather than us, because he would be furious. In actual fact he was great about it. No problem at all.

We got married in January 1966, in the registry office in Brougham Terrace, which was very well known. The locals used to call it St Brougham Teresa's. It was a great day; typical Liverpool wedding with lots of singing, dancing, drinking and of course fighting. Haha

After we got married I took Irene to live with my mum and dad, in Southport, because they had the room and we couldn't afford anything of our own. I was still only 18.

Not long after I got married I started playing in a group with George Eccles, Brent Pickthall and Barry Womersley but we couldn't settle on a name for the band; then, one day we went down to London to do some recordings for a guy called Alan Caddy. He was lead guitarist in a band called The Tornados, who backed Billy Fury and had a very big hit, in their own right, called *Telstar*. They were in fact the first British group to have a number one hit on both sides of the Atlantic. It was recorded by Joe Meek, the famous record producer.

Anyway, we went down to London to do some recording for Alan Caddy. Someone asked us the name of the band and we had to admit that we didn't, as yet, have one.

We recorded a few songs that Barry had written and which were actually pretty good but Alan said the songs were a bit too typical Liverpool. Not sure what that meant. He gave us a fiver and asked us to keep in touch. I seem to remember that it was £1, in those days to stay at The Madison so £5 was a lot of money.

Then, as we were leaving the studio someone said to us, 'The roads are all dug up around Wall St. and a lot of them are cordoned off. You'll have to go around what they're calling the *Wall St. Diversion*.'

A true lightbulb moment. We looked at each other and someone said what we were all thinking, 'What a bloody great name for a band!' and that was it. We had a name!

We didn't bother to keep in touch with Alan and later we got involved with a guy called Johnny Garfield, who was in cabaret at The Kingsway Club in Southport. He was brilliant; sang like Frank Sinatra. He'd written a few songs which were extremely good. He wrote one for the band A Taste of Honey, called *Goody Goody Gum Drops*. It was released on the RIM label and I seem to remember it did quite well.

We subsequently went to London and recorded some of Johnny's songs. One of them was called *I'll*

Cross the Road of Time. Great song but again, for no rhyme or reason it just died in the water.

My first-born, Andrew, came into the world in the May of 1966. We were at Irene's house when she went into labour. He was born at eight months. Dot, my mother-in-law, rang the ambulance as soon as she realised she was in labour. It came pretty quick and took her to the hospital. I followed it in the car. We got there in good time but still got a bollocking from a stern looking sister who for some reason thought we should have got her there sooner. Maybe she thought we could have beamed her up or something. Not sure how else we could have managed it. So, there we were, a family now, and still living at my mother's.

Wall Street Diversion disbanded in June '67 simply because people wanted to go their separate ways and do their own thing. It's inevitable with bands really.

After Wall Street Diversion split I started playing in a band called The Expressions; Les Martin, the bass guitarist, contacted me because he needed a drummer. Funnily enough their previous drummer was the same guy who had been the drummer in The Tabs before me. Pete Edge was on rhythm guitar and we also had a Hammond organ which we carried around with us.

Irene and I had moved to Liverpool by now and were living in Green Hayes Rd. It was a huge house and we rented two rooms in it. We had a living room, a bedroom with a tiny kitchen in between. We had to share the bathroom with the rest of the house, i.e.

the family who owned it and an old lady who also rented a room there. The bathroom was directly opposite our door so it wasn't pleasant. The woman of the house, as I recall, drank copious amounts of draught sherry. It really wasn't pleasant.

While I was playing in the band I also did a 9-month stint on the buses, in Liverpool. Funnily enough I had the number 60 route, which went right through where I used to live at Old Swan. All my old neighbours used to get on my bus. It was amazing to see them. I probably spent most of my shift chatting.

We had a rota of 39 duties and had to start at different times. We had to do 5 lates a month. If I was playing, and had a late on a Saturday night, I had to swap. The thing was though; to get someone to do a late on a Saturday night I had to do 2 for them during the week. Looking back, I don't know how I got away with it. I'm always being told that I'm a blagger so I suppose that was how.

We were there for the best part of 12 months. My second son, Graham, was born there. It came to a head when Irene and I had a blazing row and she left to stay with her mum. I'd got quite friendly with a policewoman. To be honest, on this occasion, friendly was all it was. There was nothing untoward going on. But for some reason she had sent me a letter which Irene got hold of. She went absolutely ballistic. She took the kids and went to her mum's.

She came back after about 3 weeks. I came home one night and couldn't get in. Then I heard the kid's inside so I banged on the door and eventually she let me in. We had another heated argument and Irene threw my case downstairs. So, this time I left and went back to my parents' in Southport.

I commuted to work for some time but it was hard. I had to get from Southport to Liverpool in time for my first shift at 5am. In the end it was too much. Eventually, I gave it up and started working for a car dealer, in Southport, driving and valeting cars; getting them ready for sale.

Irene and I made up and she brought the kids back to Southport and we lived with my mum and dad again. It hadn't been easy to live that way the first time but this time they allocated a part of the house for our own use only and that worked much better.

I still carried on playing part-time.

Alan and Irene's wedding. Courtesy of Alan Menzies

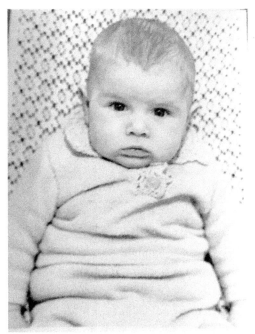

Andy aged 5 weeks. Courtesy of Irene Hume

Andy and Graham
Courtesy of Irene Hume

Jasmin T

In the autumn of 1968 Barry Womersley contacted me and asked if I would drive the band, he was currently playing in, Jasmin T, to London to do some recording. He told me he'd got this group together with drummer Barry Tweedale. Tweedale had sold his insurance business and bought a complete set of Marshall amplifiers and a drum kit. The amps were stunning, purple as I recall. In the band, at that time, were Barry Womersley (lead and vocals), John McCaffrey (bass), Barry Tweedale (drums), John Surguy (sax, flute and oboe) and Chris Hatfield (keyboard). Chris had previously played on many sessions for George Harrison. He'd played on a lot of his records.

Barry told me that, courtesy of the caretaker, the band rehearsed in the (then closed down) Palace Hotel in Birkdale when, one day, Tigon Films arrived to shoot for the film The Dark (later renamed The Haunted House of Horror). It starred Frankie Avalon, Mark Winter, Dennis Price, Richard O'Sullivan and Jill Haworth and was released in July 1969. They'd heard the band and had been very impressed with them. They'd even asked them to write the music for the opening of the film; which they did and also named that piece of music The Dark. The producer also gave them a spot in a nightclub scene, which the group wrote the music for as well.

So, they had to go down to London to record this music. By now Chris Hatfield had actually left and had been replaced by Alan Solomon on baritone sax, flute and clarinet.

I think we must have driven down on the Monday because I remember going to The Palace Hotel on the Sunday to see Tony Tenser, the producer of Tigon Films, about the expenses. He instructed his accountant to give us £10 each and another £10 for fuel; £70 in all. We thought our birthdays had all come at once. In those days bands were playing for £15 a night if they were lucky.

So, we hired a van from Avis and went down to 'town' as Tony Tenser referred to it. The lads recorded a song that Barry Womersley had written, also called *The Dark,* and they recorded an instrumental as well to be used in the club scene. They got very well paid for that too.

For some reason things weren't really working out with Barry Tweedale either and I'm not really sure why but he left. They then offered me the job and I took it.

Shortly after I joined, probably early spring '69, an agent called Derek Mac from SLA (Stewart Littlewood Associates) in Warrington, got us a recording audition with a new label called Tangerine. It was owned by businessman, Don White. He also owned a lot of bingo halls around London. We recorded five or six songs in a studio in Denmark Street including *Some Other Guy* and *Evenin'*, the old rhythm and blues number recorded by Jimmy Witherspoon. Don White was apparently blown away by *Evenin'* and signed us up. Barry was a very talented singer and to be fair he'd done an amazing job on it. I would say the contract was signed around February or March of 1969 but then the band decided to do *Some Other Guy* with a different arrangement, and we went back down to London to record that. It became the A side of the record while *Evenin'* was chosen for the B side.

In the June we got an offer to go to Germany. The gig was at The Top Ten Club on the Reeperbahn in the St Pauli district of Hamburg. It's one of the two main entertainment areas of the city though of course it's best known as a red-light district.

This would have been June '69 and we played the whole month there, from the 1st to the 30th, with a band called The Milwaukee Coasters. Their keyboard player was a 17-year-old Paul Carrack who went on to be very successful with the likes of Roxy Music and Mike and the Mechanics. He was a great song writer too and his songs have been recorded by The Eagles, Diana Ross and Tom Jones to name but a few; lovely guy as well.

Anyway, we played with them at The Top Ten Club. We went on first at 7:30 and the two bands alternated, on/off, till 4 in the morning. It was an extremely long night. Then at 10pm they used to announce, over the tannoy, that anyone under 18 had to now leave the premises. Under 18s weren't allowed in past 10 o'clock in those days.

The end of June came and the gigs ended. We did get a couple of weeks' work in Copenhagen following on from it with a company called Bendix Music. But it was a hell of a trek to get there. We had to drive from Hamburg up to Puttgarden where we got the ferry to Rodby and from there we drove to Copenhagen.

I was getting the inkling by now that Barry was

starting to get fed up with being away. He never liked to be away from home for too long. And I was right. Before we knew it, about three quarters of the way through, he'd sold his guitar to an Israeli disc jockey who was going home to back Esther Ofarim from Cinderella Rockafella fame, and the very next day he sailed home. This left us without a lead guitarist and the rest of us followed him a couple of days later.

When we got back to England our agent told us that he had a lead guitarist, called Richard (his surname escapes me for the moment) lined up for the band. He lived in Birmingham and we were asked to go and collect him, which we did. He was a great guitarist. He could also play the sitar really well. I couldn't put him up because I was still living at my parents' house with Irene and the 2 kids so he stayed with John Mac.

But at least we were able to start gigging again. Then gradually John (Saxy) and Alan (Solly) started to become discontented. They'd kept in touch with The Milwaukee Coasters and one night they offered them jobs, playing in their band. It had been reformed and renamed Warm Dust. I think they wanted to play more uncommercial stuff which Warm Dust did. They got a recording contract shortly after the guys joined them and were doing well working and living in London, which was what Saxy and Solly had always wanted.

By the autumn of '69 there was just Richard and myself left and Jasmin T had essentially broken up. Then in the November of that year, totally by chance, I met up with Barry Womersley again and he re-joined the band. Brent Pickthall was at a loose end as well so we enlisted him too.

We kept the name Jasmin T and we started playing at The Westend Club in Southport which was owned by a guy called Ray Monks who had an upholstery business downstairs. If I do say so myself, we really got that place buzzing and we played there for several months every Thursday, Friday and Saturday nights.

But that Christmas one of the guys in the band wanted to play at The Shrimper on Christmas Eve rather than The Westend Club and we did. Not really on when I think about it now but, if I remember rightly, we weren't going to get paid any extra for Christmas at The Westend Club and, of course, you did expect to get more money working over the festive season. The way they looked at it, however, was that we got paid in the slow times like January when there wasn't much money about and people didn't go out so much. I guess that was fair enough. Personally, I could live with that but not everyone was happy.

Anyway, late in the evening, on Christmas Eve, we got a phone call from The Westend Club saying that they had no music on, and could we go back there so we went. We'd done our stint at The Shrimper anyway and we ended up doing very well financially that night.

At some point in 1970 Barry decided, once more, that he wanted to leave the band and do something else and so the group broke up for the second time. Fate always seems to intervene though and not long after Brent and I were walking past The Fox and

Goose pub, in Southport, when we bumped into George Eccles (Southport is a very small place really). I asked him what he was up to and it turned out nothing much, so I invited him to come back to us, which he did.

We carried on playing The Westend Club and we also played at The British Legion, in Fleetwood, a couple of times a week. At that time Fleetwood was a big fishing port and The Legion was busy every day of the week as the guys came off the boats. It didn't matter if it was a Saturday or a Tuesday it was always heaving.

During the summer of that year The Dixieland Bar opened in Southport. The resident organist was a guy called Terry Cooper; we used to call him Mr Senior Service Cooper because he used to chain smoke Senior Service cigarettes. The drummer, Phil Mitchell, was a really good friend of mine. His nickname was Phil skins—fore an all! I still see a lot of Phil to this day and we're both still drumming, which is great.

We're now in early 1971 and George had got very friendly with the manager at The Dixieland. His name was Derek Wilson and we started doing the odd night there. In fact, Barry, Brent and myself had played at the club on one or two occasions already. Anyway, we started playing there early on Fridays, before we went to The Westend, and on Sunday lunchtimes. Then one day, it must have been February or March time, I know it was freezing cold, George asked us if we fancied playing a season at The Dixieland as he could get us an audition. Obviously, we said yes.

A guy called David Wiseman came to see us on a Sunday morning. He came from the entertainment branch of Forties, who owned The Dixieland. We did the audition in the amusement arcade at the front of the club and we got the job.

A couple of years later Wiseman told us that he personally hadn't been too sure that we could hold the job down. Apparently, it had been the manager who'd wanted us and he'd gone along with it.

'I have to say though,' Wiseman said, 'you've done a bloody terrific job. You certainly proved me wrong.' That meant a lot really.

After that we did loads of work for them. We played at the Blackpool Dixieland, the one in Morecambe and the one in Rhyl. Both the Winter Gardens at Morecambe and The Dixieland at Rhyl were struggling, and they started using us as trouble-shooters. There isn't a bigger compliment than that really when you think about it.

We still played at The Westend Club, but we didn't start there till 10:30pm. Also, we didn't need any gear for the Dixieland, we used theirs, so that helped. We used to go on there at about 9 o'clock, shoot over to The Westend to do our slot there, then back again to do another 40 minutes at The Dixieland. Then at around 12:30 it was back to The Westend to do the last spot. Oh, to be young. I feel tired even thinking about it now.

We got about £35 each a week for playing at The Dixieland but at the end of the summer season we had to re-negotiate the deal. We had been playing six nights a week but now it was the winter and so business was down. In the end the deal we managed to get for the winter months, suited us down to the ground – three nights: Thursday, Friday and Saturday (Sunday was cabaret night) for £25. Brilliant! It left us free to do other things. We usually played somewhere else on the Sunday nights and we still played The British Legion in Fleetwood on some Tuesdays and Wednesdays. We were doing great. Ann, who became my second wife, and who I'll come to later, used to run coach trips on Saturday nights, so the place rocked.

I could tell lots of tales about the goings on there, well at most clubs really. One that has stuck in mind over the years was when one of the managers got sacked for some reason and in revenge he went to one of the doormen and offered to sell him the key to the Durex machine for a fiver.

'Just don't fill it up,' he told him. 'Nobody will complain. They're too embarrassed. You go in once a week and take out the money. Bob's your uncle. It'll make you a tenner a month easy.'

So, the doorman gave him his fiver and got the key. And the manager had been right. He never filled the machine up, took the money out and no-one ever complained.

This worked really well, for several months, until the day that a bloke from Wigan overcame his embarrassment and complained, somewhat loudly, to Derek Wilson.

'Oy, there's nay fuckin' nodders int' nodder machine!'

Ooops! Well Derek was nobody's fool and he cottoned on straight away what was going on. He made some enquiries. Found out who was in charge of the key and took it off him pronto. And that was the end of that little scam. The doorman was lucky not to have been sacked as well. I've never seen anything so funny.

Around the September of 1971 Derek Wilson left and they brought in a temporary manager called Varley. He was a young trouble-shooter. Not that he needed to come trouble-shooting in Southport because that was their flagship club. In the summer season Blackpool was the only one to do better and only then; it was chokka seven nights a week but taken all year round none of them could match Southport. In the winter Blackpool was like a ghost town.

We'd already got to know Varley quite well because he used to come to our Sunday gigs. But in the November of that year he was moved from Southport to Blackpool and a new manager, called Reed, came in. For some reason, which he didn't deem necessary to tell us, Reed really didn't like us and said that at the end of the season our contract wouldn't be renewed. And it wasn't. But as one door closes . . . As soon as Varley found out that we were available he snapped us up. Reed had actually done us a big favour. So, in the January of '72, when we finished at Southport, off we went to Blackpool.

The contracts in Blackpool went from Easter to September, which was their summer season, then September to December and January to Easter. So, we were contracted to play till Easter.

It was the year of the miners' strike and the Prime Minister, Edward Heath, had introduced a 3-day week to conserve electricity and power cuts were imposed on homes and businesses. But we played all through the power cuts that year.

Varley, very cleverly, got some fairground guys to bring some generators in so we could carry on playing. We had car batteries going as well and all sorts of things. George had the amplifiers put onto 12v so they would run off the batteries. Varley also got the fairground guys to put some lights in so while everyone else was in darkness the Dixieland was open, bright and welcoming.

The place did well to put it very mildly. Why stay at home and sit in the dark with no telly when you could go to a gig and be entertained.

Then a few weeks later Varley, who used to float around for the company, was moved out and who should turn up at Blackpool but Reed. Just our fuckin' luck! Needless to say, he didn't like us any better but to his annoyance he couldn't do anything about it because we were contracted.

At the end of 1971 Irene and I broke up. It was entirely my fault. I was young, in a band and there was no shortage of girls. To put it bluntly, I couldn't keep it in my trousers. I was a bastard when I think back. Anyway, I eventually met this girl, called Ann, who I got serious with and Irene and I split.

So now I was with the girl who would become my second wife. Irene and I were still living with my mum and dad at the time, but she moved out because I wouldn't stop seeing Ann. My mate, John White, moved her out. She and the kids went into a flat. I still feel guilty about it to this day. In all honesty

I was a crap husband to both my wives and not a particularly good dad to my kids yet I have a fantastic relationship with all my children now. I'm a lucky sod in that respect and well aware that I don't deserve it.

Another thing I'm not particularly proud of, while we're on the subject, was, in my youth, getting so drunk that I couldn't play.

The Christmas before we did the season in Blackpool I'd gone to Ann's house. Her aunts, uncles and cousins were there, as well as her mam and dad, and her nan, who lived with them. So, typically, after dinner I starts drinking and drinking and drinking until I could barely stand. The problem was that I had a gig that night at The Legion. Ann managed to walk me round the block to try and sober me up a bit but I was totally pissed. In the end she had to ring Brent (Lightbulb) and tell him that I couldn't drive. Somehow, I managed to get to that gig and play even though I felt rough. As the night wore on I felt better and miraculously got through it. This time.

The second and last time was when we were in Blackpool. I'd played the first half at The Dixieland and then went to The Bernie Inn across the road. I'd had a fall out with Ann for some stupid reason and I knew she was there with her mate. I'd been drinking Bacardi all night but then I had a Pernod over the road. I actually passed out on the pavement outside the pub. Ann brought me round and I went back over to The Dixieland. I tried to play the second half, but I was well blathered. In the end a young drummer came up and finished the slot off for me.

We nearly got sacked that night because of me. Needless to say, the other band members were less than impressed. I'm ashamed to say that I blamed the doorman for lacing my drinks. Of course, he hadn't but the lie kept us our jobs.

I will never forget Brent coming to me and saying, 'Once is acceptable but twice is unforgivable.' He was right. It was totally unprofessional. I promised him there and then that it would be the last time and it was. To this day I hardly touch a drop. The odd glass of wine now and again but that's it.

Before we'd moved to Blackpool Lally Stott, of *Chirpy Chirpy Cheep Cheep* fame had come to see us a couple of times in Southport. He was originally brought to see us by Lou Fine who was a music publisher. He was a very clever guy, Lou, he knew the music business inside out. His son, Tony Fine, ended up being one of the top disc jockeys in Israel. Lally was involved with Middle of the Road and they'd had a big hit with *Chirpy Chirpy Cheep Cheep* which Lally had written in the summer of that year. Their producers subsequently thought they could do better on their own, so they left RCA. Lally thought this was a stupid move and in the end he was proved right. They did nothing more.

So, he was now looking for a replacement for Middle of the Road. He remembered me from the old days in Rhythm and Blues Incorporated and he liked me. He also liked George and Brent and the whole band in fact.

He suggested we get a girl singer so we got a girl called Sharon who was, at the time, playing with the Terry Gore Show Band. He'd got us this gig in Italy for the June after our contract at Dixieland had ended and we asked her if she'd like to come with us. She said she would, but she was only seventeen and we therefore had to get permission from her parents. We also had to get a Bow Street License for George, who was the eldest, to become her legal guardian for the duration. We finished at The Dixieland around April. By this time Ann was pregnant with our first son, David, who was born in the October of 1972.

We went over to Italy in the June as planned. We recorded quite a few songs in a studio there and we ended up getting a single release with a song called *Sands of Sahara* and *What Am I To Do* on the B side with the RCA Italiano label. It was also taken up by RCA International, which was quite something. We did several gigs in Italy. Then we started doing session work for Lally, who was still quite big over there. He'd already had a couple of really big hits.

There were a few problems with Sharon though. The rest of us had been together for years and it was hard for her to fit in. I think a lot of that was probably our fault. Also, we needed her to play the keyboard, and she was a good keyboard player to be fair, but she only wanted to play guitar all the time. There weren't many female guitarists in those days, and I think she thought it was good for her image.

Otherwise, problems that eventually emerged were ones that neither we nor Lally had really thought about though probably should have. They were personal ones. George hadn't been married long and Brent had a young son. We were away more or less permanently. The wives came out but it was still hard on them. There were also issues with Sharon being away.

In September '72 George's wife, at the time, Margaret, had been over for a visit and he ended up driving her back to England and taking Sharon with them. He came back to Italy by himself in probably late September.

We carried on and we were doing quite well, working with some pretty important people. Then David was born and I went home ,at the end of October, for a week. It made me realise what was important and when I got back it was my turn to tell the guys that it wasn't really working for me. Career wise it was great, but we were all getting fed up of being separated from our families. I suggested that we try going home, the others agreed, and we all came back to Blighty.

We got involved with an old acquaintance, called Keith Bottomley, a guitarist, who we used to work with at The Dixieland in Southport. He'd borrowed some money and moved down to South Wales with the aim of putting shows on in various venues there and he started getting us work.

We played for a number of different people including a guy called Terry Davis who was the manager of The Castle Hotel in Llandovery and eventually the Pant Yr Athro, which I'll come to. We did a lot of work for him and he became a really good friend. We often played at The Castle Hotel which was great. We used to get all our food and accommodation thrown in but in return we really drew the punters in.

If we were down in the area at any time we only had to ring him, and we could stay at the hotel for free. We often played at the Hollyland Hotel on Tuesdays. On Mondays we played somewhere else and Thursdays we played in a place called Saundersfoot. Keith actually ran his own dances there. On Fridays and Saturdays we played at various gigs around about, usually for him.

We were playing at The Castle Hotel one night when a guy called Charles Harris saw us. He was one of the directors of The Slater Walker Group who were big in the pub and hotel industry and they were getting into South Wales in a big way. He took a shine to us and we ended up playing at one of their places in Cardiganshire, as it was called at the time. We'd been playing for them for about 18 months then his company opened a brand-new chalet camp in Llansteffan, called The Pant Yr Athro. It wouldn't really be right to call it a holiday camp because it was extremely upmarket. We played there for the whole of the summer '74. We used to run everything entertainment wise even the bingo.

We had some great times down there. I learned to ride a horse. The Pant Yr Athro was in the grounds of a huge equestrian centre. I believe they were the only centre at that time to have an indoor arena outside of Wembley. It was owned by a guy called Major Buckley and his wife.

Things didn't always go according to plan, of course, even here. For instance, we played at their summer ball and The Pant Yr Athro had been promised a brick barbecue for the event but whoever had promised it to them let them down. George, Brent and I foolishly offered to build them one. What no one told us was that when you build a brick barbecue the cement has to be absolutely dry before you use it. If it isn't it tends to explode. Apparently, it should be left for a couple of weeks to dry out.

So, we built this thing in the morning and it was lit at about 6pm. Suddenly there was this God Almighty bang and people were showered with bits of brick. No-one was hurt, luckily, and so we carried on barbequing. Enough of it stayed together to allow us to somehow get the food cooked. It was a bit dangerous with bits of brick flying all over the place, but it was mighty tasty.

After the barbecue we were told that Ira, who played the harp for the Wednesday banquets, would be coming along with her choir. But then they decided the harp wouldn't be loud enough so they wanted a piano. Where at 4pm can you find a piano for a ball that starts at 7:30 that evening? Well, some bright spark said they thought that James Loving had one in his chalet. James was the manager of the equitation centre.

He did and, very foolishly, he let us borrow it. It took eight of us to carry it the 200 yards from his chalet to the spot where they wanted it.

Apart from the fiasco with the barbecue the evening went really well, and it all finished around 1am. Another good idea I'd had was to have coloured lights strung up across the yard for the summer ball and I'd mentioned this to no-one in particular a couple of days before. On the day of the ball I found a box of lights that had been left for me. I discovered later that it had been left by the chief electrician of Carmarthen. His son had overheard me say it. As it turned out they were the town's Christmas lights so they got an early airing that year.

After the ball we headed for the swimming pool up the hill where some people went skinny dipping. It was a fun night all in all.

Unfortunately, no-one was sober enough to carry the piano back and it was left on the stage. During the night, the heavens opened.

Two or three days later James asked for his piano back, so we took it back to him. We carried it back to his chalet with water literally pouring out of it. We saw him a couple of weeks later.

'That piano's making some funny noises,' he said.

Hmmm.

We used to finish playing on Saturday nights at about midnight and drive home. It took us around 3 hours. Then we'd drive back in time for the bingo on the Monday night. We also took it in turns to have Mondays off.

We played for Charles Harris through the Christmas season of 1974 as well. We played at their Christmas party at the beginning of December. All the top people came and that led to us doing one or two private dos for some of them. They lived in some absolutely amazing properties. One was like a manor house with acres of grounds. Because it was usually for the directors it didn't clash with the Pant Yr Athro and we got a lot of good spin-offs from it.

Then we did The Castle Hotel again during Christmas and New Year and had a totally full house. We started there a couple of nights before Christmas with a great disco, then did Christmas Eve, and dinner the next day. It was quite magical really. They had carol singers and a service, really nice. And, of course, we carried on with the bingo, haha. We went home the day after Boxing Day. At least Brent and I did. George was living down there by this time, so he commuted on a daily basis.

When we went back for New Year, George told us that he wouldn't be playing with us for much longer. George's wife and brother-in-law had often come down to see us play while we'd been there and George and his brother-in-law had decided to buy a pub locally. As it turned out he was quite ill in the New Year so he actually finished playing with us on New Year's Eve.

So, he left the group and stayed down there. George was always very good at blending in anywhere to be fair.

In the January of 1975 we got a guy called Terry Walters who we knew from The Dixieland to replace George and Jasmin T kept going. We played all through '75, just around and about. Nothing startling. We did some work for Derek Mac of SLA Enterprises. We used to do weeks in the working men's clubs in the north east. We were paid £350 per week so after commission we each ended up with about £90.

It was Derek who told us about an audition to go to Denmark and it was here that we would first meet Calle, who, as well as becoming our manager in Denmark, would go on to be an enormous influence in my life. His name was Carl Nielsen from CB (Calle Bookings) and Ole Bookings in Denmark. They were very trustworthy and well thought of. Believe me that was unusual in those days.

Calle came over to do the auditions and the next thing we knew we were gigging in Denmark. But there was a bit of a cock-up on the contracts. We should have gone towards the end of '75 but for some reason it didn't happen.

In the May, Terry was offered redundancy. He worked as a plant operator in Liverpool, but he really wanted to play full time, so he was delighted.

We finally went out to Denmark in June '76. We played the last 2 weeks of June there and then we went to Norway for July. The travelling was horrendous in Norway and we weren't getting that well paid to be honest. We were on £50 a day plus fuel. It wasn't unusual to do 150-200 miles in one day. We were on and off ferries and all modes of transport.

The gigs themselves were fine. Most of them were in rural church halls and that kind of thing.

One Saturday night, we hadn't picked our money up and we were a bit short. We were playing at this real hillbilly place in the middle of nowhere. We asked the guy who was running it for some money, but he told us that it was too much for him to give us. He didn't carry that much cash on him, he said. It was only then that we found out that we were earning £300 per gig. We were adamant that we weren't going on stage unless we got some of it. Well, we needed the money.

He'd booked us through a guy called Ragnor Haggen and he rang Haggen's mother who told him to pay us. So, finally, we got about £100 out of him.

Haggen wasn't best pleased when he called us the next day.

'I hear you refused to play,' he said.

'Damn right.' We told him. 'If we don't get paid, we don't play.'

Overall it wasn't a particularly nice tour. Loads of people had told us how good Norway was but there you are, we didn't find it so. To be fair we went back a few years later and it wasn't as bad that time though I still wouldn't say it was great.

After we finished, we did a week in Denmark for Calle. We played in a club called Maxim's in a place called Randers and it was chokka block every night. It was great, like going back to the '60s, but we did four 45-minute slots a night which was hard work. We didn't start till 10pm and we finished at 4 in the morning.

Calle then told us that we'd been asked to do another week. He told us we could keep the money for it and just give him his commission. Now we'd just done a month in Norway for £1,350 and he was telling us we'd end up with £620 just for this one week. I said to the other lads he's made a mistake, but he hadn't and we learned very quickly how much the agents made out of us. After that we insisted on doing it that way. In truth, it worked for him as well because if we weren't working he didn't have to pay us. It was certainly more beneficial to us even though we had to pay our own accommodation because we had work most of the time. Plus, having been there before we'd got to know people and knew where we could stay cheaply.

In late 1976 we recorded an LP at Hookfarm Studio in Copenhagen. It wasn't a massive success, but it did help us get more gigs and we sold them there.

Back then we used to play at a venue called Daddy's Dance Hall and it was there that I met a lady called Inge Nielson who worked behind the bar. Of course, the inevitable happened. At least inevitable as far as I was concerned. I started staying with her, in her flat, the result being that my daughter, Alison, was born in 1978. I somehow never learned.

We carried on playing in Scandinavia and then in 1977 Terry left us. The usual thing really. We all had families and I think Terry felt he shouldn't be away from home so much. We replaced him with Bernard Southern. We'd known Bernard for some time through various bands we'd played in.

Also, in 1977, my wife, Ann, came out with my son, David. We found a flat in Hadsund, in Denmark, and she got a job as a barmaid at a local disco. We knew the manager, Anni Hjortlund, and she is still a very good friend today. Ann couldn't speak a word of Danish, but it didn't matter. Anni would just shout beer, or whatever, to her and Ann would pour it. She really enjoyed it. We were playing regularly, and things were going really good for us. We ended up staying in Denmark until 1982.

We played in Copenhagen quite often and I continued staying with Inge when we were there. Alison was born in February '78. In the end Inge and Ann were pregnant at the same time and my youngest, Howard, was born in the August of '78. I'm not proud of my behaviour at all but at the same time I wouldn't be without any of my kids so . . .

Ann didn't want Howard to be born in Scandinavia and went back to England to have him. By that time, we'd started playing in The Faroe Islands and in Norway anyway so we weren't in Denmark that much. Ann had originally come out because she hadn't liked being on her own in England but she'd just ended up being on her own in Denmark.

We actually had a number one hit in The Faroe Islands. A song called *Faroe Girl*, written by Ivan Pedersen, who was Calle's drummer. He later became very big in Denmark as part of a duo called Laban. The B side of *Faroe Girl* was a number called *Rock and Roll Music*. Calle had got us the recording contract. We made the record, pressed it and distributed it. It sold out.

Something worth mentioning about the clubs in The Faroes; back then while the islands were essentially dry, if you paid your taxes you got a quota of alcohol. Clubs were set up and were run on a strict membership basis and they took the alcohol quota of their members. They would have bingo nights and entertainment etc., it gave people some incentive to pay their taxes I guess, lol.

So, Brent, Bernard and myself were doing very well. We sold a lot of albums and everywhere we played was heaving. There was no beer there back in those days. You had to make your own. There was no TV either and everything on the island stopped at 6:30 in the evening while everyone listened to the news on the radio. At the end of the news they would announce where we were playing.

One of the places we played in was a huge tin hut, built on stilts, which protruded over the sea. I heard it fell into the water eventually. The roads were always totally gridlocked with people getting to and from the gig. We used to finish off the night with red and blue indoor fireworks. Our roadie, Tommy, used my drum case to stand them on. I still have red and blue stains on that drum case to this day, 40 years on.

Tommy is no longer with us unfortunately. He got killed on a motorway in Denmark. He was walking on the hard shoulder, having run out of petrol, and was run over by a drunk driver. Only a young guy too. Very sad.

I went home when Howard was born. We all took 3 weeks off and I had every intention of spending it with the family. But, of course, my life changes by the hour. It still does to this day.

Ann had Howard in the early hours of the Sunday morning. On the Monday the phone rings; it's Calle, 'You need to get back right away,' he says. 'I've got a £2,500 deal here, with Montax. They want a country and western tape doing pronto.'

Montax was an independent record label but mainly produced cassettes. There was no tax on cassettes in Denmark at that time.

So, we all flew back the next day. That went down really well at home as you can imagine. It was this sort of thing that probably goes a long way to explaining why I've been married and divorced twice. Well, one of the things.

We knocked the album out in a few days and I asked the other lads if they would mix it while I went back to England. Bernard wasn't too happy at first because he was worried that I might not like how they did it. But after some assurances they were okay, and I went back to England. The flight back was a 'where were you when?' moment for me. I'll never forget that when I got on the plane, that day, I heard that Keith Moon had died.

Then Calle got us a recording contract with CBS, in Denmark. It was a song that Brent, our bass player, had written called *Wait A Minute. I'm Not in Love*, written by 10cc was the B side. It didn't reach no. 1 but it did very well. It was Christmas time and I remember a guy called Sebastian who was very popular there at the time, also brought out a record and we sold more than him; which was amazing in the circumstances. He wasn't very happy, but we were and it certainly raised the profile of the band.

One time when we played in the Faroes, Brent and Bernard sailed there, with our 2 roadies, from Scrabster to Torshavn, but I decided I would fly. So, I flew to Denmark, stayed the night with Inge and then got a plane with Maersk Air to The Faroes. Now of course in those days it was all sight landing there. They had no radar at the airport and to make matters worse it was down in a valley. This was a Thursday and we were playing that night. Of course, the weather sets in and we can't land. Bernard and Brent are at the venue, ready to do the gig, and no drummer. Luckily, there was this little guy, called Oscar, who played with one of the local bands and they got him to play with them. Oscar saved the day to be fair. I was able to get there for the gig the following night and we did the rest of the tour without a hitch.

In 1980 it all started to fizzle out a little though we still did a fair bit playing around Denmark and Norway.

Then a guy called Phil Barrett came over with his band, The Child's Play. He got romantically involved with a very good friend of ours called, Benta. I had been lodging with Benta since Ann went back to the UK. Phil then moved in with her. He joined the band and we became a foursome again. We then started doing Beatles numbers. We got the suits and everything.

And so began another chapter in our musical career.

Left to right Barry Womersley, Alan Menzies, John Surguy,
Alan Solomon, John McCaffrey.
Record cover of Some Other Guy/Evenin' designed by John
McCaffrey. Tangerine Records

Courtesy of Adam Yaffe – Yaffe Photography

Left to right George Eccles, Alan Menzies, Brent Pickthall
Courtesy of Adam Yaffe – Yaffe Photography

From left to right: Alan Menzies, Sharon Emery,
George Eccles, Brent Pickthall

Alan, Howard, Ann and David
Courtesy of Anni Hjortlund

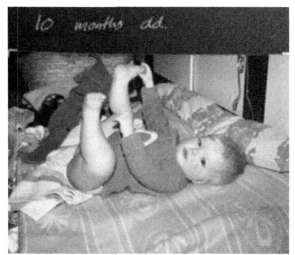

Alison. Courtesy of Alan Menzies

The Bootles

So, in 1980 I was playing in Denmark, Sweden and Norway with Phil Barrett, Bernard Southern and Brent Pickthall (Lightbulb). To start with we were doing a mixture of 10cc stuff and Beatles songs. We greatly admired The Beatles, both in their writing and music, and it seems that everyone else did too. It didn't matter how many Beatles songs we played, loads of people would always come up and ask us to do more.

Then we had this idea – why didn't we just play Beatles stuff, well predominantly anyway. But we thought we needed a new name. We brain-stormed each other and we all threw names into the mix. Eventually we somehow came up with The Bootles. Everyone loved it. We went to management with the idea and the new name and they thought it was brilliant.

We had four Beatle suits made, the collarless ones and Sergeant Pepper suits. They were made by the wife of a disc jockey, Daniel, we knew out there. They were magnificent, especially the Sergeant Pepper ones. We had a photo session and started promoting the band. Calle organised a huge mail shot all over Scandinavia. We recorded an album of Beatles songs and away we went. Almost overnight our money went up from £300 to £800 per gig and that was just playing two spots instead of the four we had been playing. Things were looking up again.

We went down really well in Norway. We played at the Norwegian army bases Monday to Thursday. We went on at 7:30, in our collarless suits, and did all the old songs up to 1966. The sessions were 45 minutes so we'd come off at 8:15, have half an hour's break, change into our Sergeant Pepper suits, and go back to do the Sergeant Pepper set.

These concerts were free to the troops and, as is often the case with things that are gratis, they hadn't been really appreciated or well attended. But for some reason we got known and word spread. After a while we were playing to packed houses. Sometimes American troops came over, on secondment, to do exercises with the Norwegian military. They would come to the gigs and they really loved us.

It was while we were there that we had a horrendous car crash and we were very lucky to get out alive. We were travelling in the van, up to a tunnel, on our way to Honningsvag and the road up to the tunnel looped so you couldn't actually see into it until you got there.

I was driving and as soon as I entered it, I saw a bulldozer about 20 feet in front. These tunnels were only the width of two cars so it was totally blocking it. The bulldozer was crawling onto the back of a low loader. Unbelievably, it turned out that they were doing this inside the tunnel because it was such a slow process and it was raining outside. They didn't want to get wet!

On the back of the bulldozer there was an arm sticking out with a hook hanging down from it. Everything seemed to happen in slow motion but I realised instantly that I wasn't going to stop. Brent was sitting in the middle of the front seat and I knew that if the hook came through my windscreen it would have killed him. I swerved to the right running the left front wheel up the low loader's ramp. This enabled me to just miss the hook. The back of the arm hit the windscreen and the van jammed between the low loader and the side of the tunnel.

Remarkably no-one was hurt but the van was undriveable because the steering box and front axle were damaged.

Fortunately, we were in a Scandinavian vehicle rescue service called Falck. We contacted them and they came and put the van on the back of a rescue vehicle. They actually took us to our gig even though it was on another island. We had to get a ferry to it; rescue guys an' all. We got there slightly late but at least we got there and were able to play. They'd really gone the extra mile and we were very grateful to them.

The next day a guy on the island, who had a little transport company, took us to Hammerfest for the next gig. He also took the van to the Ford dealers in Hammerfest. We were pretty grateful to him too.

We had five or six gigs left to do but we couldn't do them as we didn't have a vehicle and the cost of hiring one would have been prohibitive. We left our gear with the owner of the club, in Hammerfest, and flew back to Denmark. We got in touch with the insurance agent, who we knew quite well, and he informed us that it would be at least five to six weeks before the Ford dealer could fix it.

It was impossible that we could wait so long, as we still had dates to fulfil back in Denmark, so I offered to go back up to Hammerfest myself and repair it. He told me that would be okay.

There was a salvage yard about five miles from where we lived where they dismantled late model vehicles. As luck would have it he had a Ford Transit van, the same year as ours, and it'd had a rear end crash. The front axle and steering box were in immaculate condition so we bought it. We lived in Hadsund, which was about 1,400 miles (1900 km) from Hammerfest and getting there was like organising a military operation. Lightbulb took me to the local airport, Aalborg, where I flew to Gothenburg in Sweden then on to Oslo in Norway, from there to Tromso, then Lakselv and finally to Hammerfest. It took me about twelve hours.

The Ford garage was next door to the airport, much to my relief as I had a front axle and steering box and they were no lightweight. The airport had a little electric cart and they very kindly transported it into the garage for me in that. It was quite late when I arrived but the garage owner was still there. He was a bit peeved that I was going to do it myself because it would have been a good job for them. In fact, he wasn't going to let me do it at first but when I pointed out that the van couldn't be moved in its present state he finally agreed to me doing it albeit outside of working hours. The insurance agent had told me that he would lend me hydraulic jacks and tools etc. but he definitely wasn't up for that.

I had a toolkit and the screw jack in the back of the van so I made a start straight away doing what I could. I used a large rock to hold up one side and the screw jack to hold up the other. I started around 7pm and by 10:30 I had it all stripped down ready for the new parts to go on. Of course, being summer, it was

77

still broad daylight. For some reason the boss came back just as I'd finished. I could see the look of astonishment on his face as he drove past. I don't think he thought I could do it.

I stayed with a mate, Kai, in Hammerfest that night and went back to the garage the next afternoon to finish off. To my amazement the owner's attitude had totally changed. He couldn't do enough for me. He blew the tyre up and I bought some brake pads from him. I resumed work at about 4pm and by 10:30 the job was pretty much done but the battery was flat so I couldn't start it till the next day when Kai came and gave me a jump start. I had been so engrossed in what I was doing I hadn't seen that a herd of reindeer had surrounded me and were totally mesmerised in what I was doing. Amazing sight. One of those things that never leave you.

When I went in to fill up the guy who served me said, 'You have my boss's respect. He couldn't believe what you'd achieved in two nights with minimal tools.' I guess that explained his change of attitude towards me. I was quite chuffed really.

It was also during this time, and again because of the van, that I caught my first sight of the northern lights. It was a dark, very cold, frosty night and we were driving to one of the military gigs in Lakselve, North Norway, when the engine started to knock. I was dozing until Lightbulb, who was driving, said 'Hey Al, is this engine trying to cease up?'

'Whoa,' I said, 'pull over, stop! You're gonna fuckin' blow it up.'

So, we pulled over and I was looking under the bonnet when one of the guys just says, 'Fucking hell look at that.'

And we all looked up at the sky. My God what a sight it was. Now I'm known more for my profanities than being poetic but they were like vertical, shimmering lights, like spotlights reaching into heaven. They looked like they were dancing around in the darkness; as though they were searching for something in the pitch-black sky. They lasted for some moments and then simply disappeared. We were awestruck. Something else I'll never forget.

I couldn't do anything with the engine though. It was pretty much Donald Ducked but it would still run to a fashion. We were still about 100 miles from the gig. I took over the driving and nursed it the rest of the way. It must have taken 4 hours to do, uphill, down dale and around mountains.

But we finally made it at around 5 o'clock in the morning and parked up outside the Ford dealer. They used to start work at 7:30 so we hung around. When they opened up, I went in and enquired about getting a new engine. They said they could have one flown in from Oslo the next day and could complete the work by the day after at the latest.

The army camp wasn't far away so we limped it up there. I spoke to the officer in charge and explained to him that although we had made this gig we wouldn't be able to get to their concert in Kirkenes, which was around a couple of hundred kilometres away, because we didn't have a van.

He said, 'Tell you what, if you pay for the petrol, I'll get one of my drivers to take you up in one of our vehicles.'

So, we played the gig and the next morning we

loaded our gear into their van. I dropped ours off at the Ford Dealers with the army guy, Chelsea, following me. We then set off for Kirkenes in his vehicle.

I remember we stopped on the way at a transport cafe and told Chelsea to order anything he wanted and we'd pay. We really must have been grateful, lol. We thought he would order a nice juicy steak or something but instead he orders kjottekake which is meat rissoles with boiled spuds. It's a Norwegian staple diet which he almost certainly got in the army at least twice a week.

We finally got to the camp in Kirkenes and set up our gear. We couldn't stay on the camp for security reasons, so Chelsea took us into the town where we found a hotel. We played that night and loaded up the gear afterwards so that we didn't need to do it in the morning. Chelsea dropped us off at the hotel and arranged to pick us up at 10 the next morning. When he arrived he had another guy from the camp with him who asked us if we wanted to see the Russian border. We didn't need to be back in Lakselv for the van till 4pm and it was only a few kilometres out of Kirkenes so we said 'Great!'

There was a river running between Russia and Norway but there was also a land border which at the time was heavily guarded. There were watch towers every hundred yards or so on the Russian side. We were taken to a Norwegian one. These were fewer, maybe 250 yards apart, and we all climbed the steps to get up to the top. It was very basic but it didn't seem to be operational. I don't think we really should have been there to be honest but it was really interesting. The guys gave us binoculars to look over the river at the Russian towers. They certainly were operational and strangely I felt a bit sorry for the guys in them. They were open to all the elements. I asked the Norwegian blokes why they had so many towers on the Russian side and he told me they would shoot anybody who tried to swim across. As I was looking over at the towers, I could see a Russian soldier looking at me. I mentioned this to one of the Norwegian guards and he said he'd been clocking me since we first climbed up.

'Fuck him,' he said.

The journey back to Lakselv was more or less the same as the trip up. We stopped to eat, and Chelsea had something different but again nothing special despite being invited to. When we got to the army base we paid them for the petrol. They told us the Ford garage had been on to say our van was ready so Chelsea took us down there and we loaded the gear into our van and went to pay our bill. Of course, there are always extras that weren't in the quote and which we hadn't budgeted for and we were about £200 short. Luckily this was the early eighties. We explained we didn't have any more money until we'd played that night at a club about seventy miles away. The guy rang the club and spoke to the owner who spoke to us. He asked if it was ok to pay the garage on our behalf after we'd played. We agreed to that, so the garage gave us the van and we all said thanks for the super service and drove off to the gig. We couldn't believe how trusting they were, but we did the gig; the club owners paid them the next day and all was well. Imagine going into a Ford, or any garage, today, being £200 short and driving away.

Musically we were riding high. It was nothing to go over to Norway for a month and play every night. We would do the bases Monday to Thursday and then other gigs at the weekends. But even at the weekends we would never play beyond 1am. This was so unlike Denmark where it was nothing to be expected to play till 4am. It seems it was thanks to The Musician's Union which was very strong in Norway at the time

Calle had a Turkish contact called Kamille who was very well in with the Eastern Block TV. Around the autumn of 1980 he got us a deal with him doing a TV spectacular but we wouldn't get cash. Instead we would get two full price, open air tickets from Denmark to UK with Scandinavia Airlines. This was common practice in those days. The tickets were valid for a year and you could change the names on them. I sold one of mine to Brent. The shows were Christmas and New Year Specials and we flew out on a Sunday, I would say October time, from Copenhagen to Vienna where we had a four-hour stopover till the next flight to Sofia in Bulgaria where the TV show was being recorded.

As we had 4 hours to kill we took a bus into Vienna to have a look around. It was lovely; a lot of families out and about though being Sunday there wasn't much open. We had coffee in a Viennese café in one of those magnificent European squares. It was amazing but also very expensive and we hadn't changed that much money, so we got the bus back to the airport.

When it was time for our flight (we were flying the second leg with Balkan (Bulgarian Airlines)) we were bussed to the far side of the airport to a very old Russian Tupolev, yikes! But it was full to bursting; every seat was taken. Calle was 6 foot and there was so little space between the seats his legs were in the aisle. They then brought some plastic trays out with some meat on. Well I think it was meat. It looked like meat but it tasted like nothing I'd ever tasted before. I didn't eat it and anybody who knows me knows it must have been grim for me not to eat it. They then offered some form of cake which was so sweet it would've given you a sugar rush. Finally came the tea/coffee, whatever you wanted as long as that was a tea bag in a plastic cup or a sachet of Nescafe. The hot water came from a kettle the likes of which your grandma would have used. You know the type, you heat the water on a hob and have to use a tea towel or something to hold the handle because it's so hot. They came round and proceeded to pour the boiling water on to our tea/coffee. Health and Safety was unheard of in those days. They'd have had a field day.

After the meal there was an announcement over the sound system. It was in either Bulgarian or Russian so none of us understood a word, but we saw that people weren't happy. We eventually found out through other passengers and several languages that Sofia was fog bound.

We eventually landed at an airport about 300 miles from Sofia and what a culture shock that was. It was like something out of a Harry Lime film very grey and very drab. We were ushered into a room and told we would be bussed to Sofia sometime the next day. Kamille went mad saying we had to be at the TV studio the next day and was there anybody who could help us get a couple of taxis?

While we were trying to sort transport out an American guy came up to us and said, 'You guys seem to be the only ones here that speak English.'

He was an orchestra conductor who was guest conducting the Sofia equivalent of our Philharmonic Orchestra and he was due at rehearsals the next morning at ten. He asked if he could possibly share a taxi with us and of course we agreed. We had two cars and he made eight altogether; Calle, Kamille, myself and a record executive from a Danish record company as well as the rest of the band so we had a spare seat albeit a bit cramped.

When the Bulgarian drivers arrived, they were reluctant to take us all that way but after ringing the hotel in Sofia and speaking to the manager they agreed to do it.

We set off probably around 10 or 11 pm. There were no motorways only what we would class as B roads. It was very dark and dismal. Calle was in the front car and I was in the one following with Kamille and the American conductor. The journey seemed to go on for hours and I think we got to the Hotel in Sofia at around 4 to 5 am. The manager came out and started talking to the drivers and Kamille. We had driven 300 miles and they asked for the equivalent of £130 each. Kamille told the manager to give them $200 each, which was worth another third in their own currency, but they were very cagey about taking it. It was illegal for them to take any other currency than Bulgarian but the manager convinced them that nobody would know so two very happy guys started their drive back home after a hearty breakfast. The hotel was a Japanese owned 5* so we were also happy campers.

None of us had eaten for hours so Kamille got us all in the lobby where we were checking in and told us to meet him in his room if we wanted to eat. I think one or two went to bed but most of us went and he rang room service. It was roughly 5am in the morning and the guy who arrived to take our order took one look at us all and you could see the shock register on his face. He explained he was on his own and it would be at the very least an hour and half before we would get any food. It only took a 20$ note, however, to secure 6 omelettes and chips in 15 mins and then straight to bed. Luckily, we didn't have to get up till 11am as we didn't have to be at the TV studio till 2pm.

The studio was in the city centre and, as we drove through, it was quite surprising to see women working alongside men digging roads and road cleaning etc:

We got there and started putting the shows together for the Christmas and New Year. We had an interpreter with us. I got quite friendly with a makeup lady and after a couple of days I invited her, through the interpreter, back to our hotel to join us for drinks and dinner. She said she'd absolutely love too but didn't dare as fraternising with westerners was frowned upon. If she was found with us her name would be put on a register and, if found again, she could be fined a year's wages. She had a very good job and didn't want to jeopardise it. I was quite shocked by that but, of course, it was another world.

On one of the days, after filming, we went to a record shop in Sofia with a representative of Balkon records who had pressed our Bootles' cassette (the one we'd made in Denmark) on to an LP record. We didn't know what the quality would be like, but we were pleasantly surprised; it was great. The shop was huge and full of classical music records. You could buy things like the complete works of Rachmaninoff by the Moscow Philharmonic for £40.

And there was our LP stood next to the other pop LPs. It was standing proudly amongst the likes of ABBA, Elton John, Smokey and Cliff Richard. The rep said it had been on the shelves for only three weeks and had already sold around 80,000 copies. By the time the New Year's Eve show went out they expected to sell another 30,000; and after the broadcast another 70,000-80,000. The program was set to be repeated around Easter time when they estimated they would probably sell another 40,000-50,000 copies. So, all in all we were looking at sales in excess of quarter of a million. This show was broadcast in all Eastern Bloc countries and this was nine years before the Berlin Wall came down, so the potential audience was many millions. But hey, surprise, surprise, they didn't recognise western performing rights, so we got absolutely nothing from record sales and neither did John, Paul, George or Ringo for that matter and it was their songs we recorded. Still, they could afford the loss more than us, lol.

We were leaving Bulgaria on the Thursday but

there was thick fog and nothing was flying. We were due to finish filming in the hotel lobby around 2pm and we were told the fog had lifted slightly and to get to the airport pronto, like in the next ten minutes. We all rushed to our rooms and just threw everything into our cases and away we went. When we got to the airport there was good news. There was an Austrian Air flight to Vienna and we managed to get on it.

We took off just as the fog was coming in again. It wasn't till we were halfway to Vienna that I realised I'd left all my Beatle clothes in the wardrobe. Shit! You can imagine the names I was called by the others.

A seamstress in Southport, called Barbara, made me another Sgt Pepper suit and I had another Beatle suit made from a local tailor in Denmark.

All in all, it was quite an experience.

Another time we had a gig in a ski resort in Geilo, in Norway. We were playing there at night but arrived during the afternoon when there was a fashion show on. This meant we couldn't get our gear in. It was on the side of a mountain and there was an atomic bomb shelter which held around 400-500 people. This of course was the right in the middle of the Cold War, and we were close to the Russian border so the shelter was always open. As it had all the facilities, like toilets etc. they were using it as changing rooms.

The guys were at the bar and I was in the back talking to the people who were putting on the fashion show. Suddenly I noticed this suspender belt and picked it up.

Jokingly one of the ladies said 'Is that your size?'

'If I had some stockings, I'd go out on the catwalk in it and just my underpants,' says I.

They all fell about laughing, then to my horror the boss said, 'If you're serious, I'll give you a bottle of whiskey if you do.'

Now this whiskey cost £50 a bottle, so naturally I agreed to do it. We didn't have any stockings so a woman takes off her black tights, cuts the top off and gives me the two legs. So, I stripped off till all that was covering me was my underpants and put on the makeshift black stockings and a suspender belt.

The compere announced a new line in ladies' lingerie and I strolls onto the catwalk. The place was packed and it just erupted with laughter. I could hear our guitarist, Phil, laughing above everyone else and there were about 300 people there.

Most of them stayed on for dinner and the evening show. The boss said that Sunday nights were usually very hit and miss because of people having to be at work the next day. But most stayed and I like to think that it was my little escapade which helped to achieve those numbers. He gave us a free meal and true to his word a bottle of whisky. As I don't drink it the rest of the band were really made up.

Norway lasted about eighteen months but like all good things it eventually came to an end. Austerity kicked in, in the early 80s, and of course the first thing to go was the troops' entertainment. And, consequently, our gigs.

But during this time our manager, Calle, was bringing bands and solo artists over from England as well as from all over Europe. One particular singer was a Dutch girl called Xandra who'd had a very big hit called Colerado in Denmark. Calle put us on tour with her and she used our sound equipment. Xandra's boyfriend was a guy called Ferdie Bolland who was half of the duo, B and B, his brother, Rob Bolland, being the other half. They were virtually unknown in England but massive on the continent. They had a huge hit with a record, which they wrote themselves, called *In the Army Now*. Status Quo subsequently had a hit with it in England.

For some unknown reason Xandra didn't re-sign with her Danish record company so Calle decided to sign her up to his, Blue Records, and he started recording her. On the second day of recording the session drummer couldn't make it so Calle asked me to step in. I ended up playing on the A side of the record, which was called *America Here I Come*.

After the tour came to an end Ferdie and Xandra liked us so much they offered to get us some work in Holland doing 'The Beatles Stuff'.

And they did! We arrived in Rotterdam on a Thursday evening ready to start work on the Friday. Then Rob Bolland arrived at the hotel mid-morning to tell us he'd got us on a TV show that evening. It was a program called Sonia's Good News and it was a topical magazine show. There'd been a lot of trouble over the last couple of months between the musician's union and TV companies about the use of playback. As a result, all artists had to play live from this show on.

We were really nervous and then, just as we went live, the floor manager said to us, 'Good luck, guys.

There are 12 million people watching you.' That really didn't help!

Luckily, we didn't play a single wrong note and, to our immense relief, everything went well. But because of the TV show we were late for our first scheduled gig. As luck would have it, it turned out the promoter hadn't advertised the gig that well and not many people had actually turned up so he wasn't that upset. It had given him the perfect excuse to cancel it. We still did the Saturday and Sunday gigs though and they were great; well-advertised and well attended.

Calle's nephew, Tommy, was our roadie. I remember after the Sunday gig, which finished at about 4am, we were loading the gear into the van when Tommy comes up with one of the bins (speaker cabinets) which are big and heavy. Somebody had thrown up outside and of course Tommy had to step in it. And he goes flying; arse over tit.

It was raining too and quick as a flash Lightbulb yells 'Don't let that bin touch the floor, Tommy!'

So poor Tommy ends up on his back, on the wet ground, with the bin on his chest. He couldn't move and was pleading with us for help but all we could do was stand around pissing ourselves laughing. Eventually we managed to compose ourselves enough to give him a hand and, luckily, he was none the worse for wear.

At the end of the weekend we were owed 2,000 guilders (about £800) and a guy, called Jan, who worked for the booking agency said he would come after the Sunday gig to pay us. Well, it got to about 4:15am and we were ready to go, and frankly getting a bit anxious, when he finally turned up. He pulled out a wodge of money that would choke a horse, peeled off 2,000 guilders and gave them to us.

It turned out he was late because he'd been closing a deal with Tom Jones's management for 55,000 dollars and there was us panicking about 2,000 guilders. How the other half live, eh!

We carried on playing across Scandinavia and we were still earning quite good money but there was a sameness about it all and we didn't really feel that we were making any progress. We were offered an amazing gig in South Africa playing the Hilton Hotels in Cape Town, Johannesburg and Sun City. The money was astounding and legally tax free. We were offered the equivalent of £550 per week plus all expenses. That would be worth well over £2,000 today. The crunch was it was a six-month stint and Brent was in a newish relationship and Phil had just married his second wife, Bente. Needless to say, they were none too keen on spending that length of time away and they flatly refused to go, so sadly, we had to let the opportunity pass us by.

Finally, at Christmas 1982, Bernard and I decided to go home to England. Brent and Phil, of course, had their Danish wife and girlfriend and had houses in Denmark so they stayed on. That turned out to be short lived for Brent however and he brought his girlfriend back to England, where they got married, about 18 months later.

Bernard, Brent and myself carried on playing the clubs, in England as The Bootles, even though there were only three of us. We'd got in touch with Ricky

McCabe, the agent, again and he got us a lot of work locally.

Then in 1983 we struck lucky. Around the April of that year Stan Irben, a great rock and roll pianist, who we knew from Denmark, got in touch with me with a view to playing in Ibiza. At that time he lived there.

A Dutch guy called Ryan Munthangen owned a club called Sgt Pepper's in San Antonio Bay and he wanted two bands to provide the entertainment. He split the season for us because it normally ran from Easter until the middle of October, which was around 32 weeks, and none of us wanted to do that long.

He told me he'd heard of this band called Gaz and the Groovers and he was coming over to England to see them. Now my guys weren't around at that particular time, so he says,

'I'm going to take a big chance on The Bootles. I've heard a lot of great things about the band and I'm willing to take you based on your reputation. You'll be the first ever band I've booked without seeing.'

I was bowled over. That was some compliment.

Unfortunately, in the end, we couldn't do the first part of the season for him anyway because we were already committed in Norway for the whole of June, So, he split the season. Gaz and Groovers did the first half till mid-July then we did the rest.

Terry re-joined us but that time scale caused a problem for him. He worked for Fisher's Carpets in Leigh and, to be fair, his boss was a really great, tuned in guy and he'd already given him 13 weeks off to do Ibiza.

'Look guys,' Terry said, 'I can't really take the piss and take a month off, go back for a couple of weeks and then take another three and a half months off.'

And we totally understood but we were going as The Beatles and obviously had to go as a four-piece. There was this young guy called Ian James who we'd used in the past. He could play both rhythm and bass guitar, though we only needed him to play rhythm, and we took him with us to Norway. He was only about 17 years old and he'd just had a hernia operation. The wound was literally 14 days old, so we had to be really careful in not letting him lift anything etc. But we did the whole month with Ian, all over Norway, and, believe me, it was nothing to do two or three hundred miles a day in Norway. He bore up well. We were proud of him.

We then went back to England for a couple of weeks, Terry re-joined us and, once again, we started playing around and about at the local clubs.

In the middle of July, we went to Ibiza. We started on a Saturday and we played four spots a night. The first spot we wore the collarless Beatles jackets and did their early stuff up to '67. In the second spot we came on as ourselves and did a variety of stuff. The third set we wore our Sgt Pepper suits and obviously played tracks from 1967 onwards, including lots of numbers from the album. In the final spot we came on as ourselves again. Other musicians would often get up and jam with us on the last spot.

The sets weren't long, to be fair, only about 35/40 minutes but the gig would go on all night. There was a guy called Kevin, who played guitar, and we alternated with him. He would go on first and we would end the night. Our first spot would be about 10:40pm and we would finish around 4 in the morning. Actually, we were supposed to finish at 3 but in high season he would stretch it out. We weren't thrilled about that but we went along with it. We just took longer breaks during the night.

After about a month, the suits were getting ruined because of the heat in the club so we stopped wearing them although we still played the same spots. This did once get us into a bit of trouble. A guy who'd seen us play early in the season when he'd been there on holiday, was really disappointed that we weren't wearing them. He'd come back and brought some mates with him to see us. I don't think he really understood when I tried to explain why. He was seriously hacked off because he'd told his friends about us and brought them over. Unfortunately, as far as he was concerned, we were doing something different. We weren't really doing anything different at all. We just weren't wearing the suits, but I still felt bad about it.

About ten weeks into it, Terry started to get fed up. Usual thing, he didn't want to be away from home for too long. The problem was we still had three weeks to do.

It was around then, probably about the third week in September, that Ryan got me in the office. Now he had a certain reputation so I knew what was coming. Basically, he wanted us to carry on doing what we were doing but for less money. We had air tickets to go home the middle of October. He reminded me, once again, that he was paying us more than anyone else on the island and I reminded him, once again, that there was a reason for that.

'I can't afford to keep paying you this money,' he said. 'Things are starting to drop off.'

Funnily enough no one else had noticed trade was dropping off.

He was paying us about £35 each a night, which admittedly was a lot back then. We worked seven nights a week so that worked out at £245. Our accommodation was also paid so we only had to feed ourselves.

'Ah, well I have a solution,' I told him. 'Bernard, Brent and I usually operate as a three-piece. Terry isn't a permanent member of the band and he's pretty much ready to go home. We could carry on as a three-piece till the end of the season. That way you're saving £35 a night straight away.'

Well Ryan was never one to be beaten.

'Okay,' he says 'but I can only pay you £30 a night from now on.'

'Fair dos, but we finish at 3am.'

And we agreed on that.

So, Terry went home. He got a cheap flight because we were quite well in with all the holiday reps on the island, especially those from Buddies, 18-30 and 20s. I think it was John from Twenties who got him the flight.

All the reps used to come into our club and the club looked after them because they would bring forty or fifty people in, and they, being holiday makers, would spend a lot of money.

I got really friendly with one of their reps. Her name was Jo and I got quite involved with her. She lived on the other side of the bay to San Antonio. Now Jo used to drink a lot, to put it mildly, and it got to the stage where the taxi drivers wouldn't take her home. Not that she was sick in their cabs or kicked off or anything but she wouldn't pay them. In the end she got such a reputation that if we were waiting for a taxi after a night out or a gig I had to hide her or they wouldn't stop. Then when they finally realised she was there they would attempt to drive off and I would have to hang on to the car while I assured them that they would get paid. There wasn't even much in it for me in the end. I'd get her home and put her to bed but by the time I'd got around to getting into bed myself she'd be totally flaked out. Such is life.

I used to do beach parties for Buddies at Santa Eulalia. I borrowed a guitar from a friend of mine called John Williamson who did a solo spot at one of the bars. It was really good money but I remember confiding in Terry when I first started, that I didn't know if I'd overstepped the mark by taking on a beach party on my own. I didn't feel that my guitar skills were really that good.

Terry said, 'You'll be fuckin' fine, Big Al. Just play everything in C.'

And everything was fine without resorting to Terry's advice. I would get the same for doing one hour as I did for a whole evening at the club. Their manager, Marian, used to pick me up and drive me to Santa Eulalia. We would often see Terry Thomas walking about because, of course, he used to live there.

Brent and I also did a gig for Twenties. They had

an organised excursion for their holiday-makers. It started at about two in the afternoon when they were taken on a 45- minute boat ride to this island. We would go with them. Once there they played games and stuff like that. Then there would be dinner after which Brent and I would play for about forty minutes. We did this every week. You could get away with a lot more with Twenties and we used to play all sorts of racy songs that you couldn't do with Marian. She was a bit strait-laced really. It was a lot of fun though.

At the end of the season Jo, and some of her colleagues, left about a week before we did. I went on the bus to the airport with them. I remember

her saying that she hoped it wouldn't just be a holiday romance, but I think we both knew we would never see each other again. I did say that I would go to some of their reunions and I meant it at the time. They even tried to book us to play at them once or twice but, for some reason, either one or the other member of the group couldn't do it and unfortunately it never happened. Plus, we all lived in the North West and the reunions tended to be down in London so that didn't help.

Bernard, Brent and myself came back to England mid-October 1983. Terry re-joined us and, once again, we carried on playing Beatles stuff as a four-piece band.

At the time, however, Bernard's brother was quite high up in the Barratt Housing company and Bernard got himself a full-time job selling properties. So, in early '84 he left us to do a 'proper job' and we continued yet again as a three-piece.

We more or less went back to playing part time for a while and doing the odd gig in Denmark. Terry returned to work at Fisher's and Brent was doing odd jobs. I had a rented unit in Birkdale fixing cars.

Phil was still in Denmark. He was doing a lot of work for Puk Studios and he played with some big names. In fact, Elton John later recorded at that studio. I think it was number three of the top studios in the world at one time. The problem was that it was in the wrong place. It was just outside Randers, in the middle of nowhere, and in the winter, you pretty much needed a tractor to get to it. Nevertheless, he got us a lot of work when we were in Denmark but in the end he and his family came back to England too.

We carried on going over about once a year for a week to ten days but we obviously needed to be a four-piece to do Beatle's music. As Phil wasn't always available we took a friend of ours called John Williamson to play lead guitar.

Dougie Martell, the DJ, got us work, as did Calle. The rest of the time we were playing round the clubs in Liverpool, Bolton and around the North West generally.

We also did two summer seasons for Pontins in Morecambe and Blackpool. The entertainments manager was a guy called Ken Skelton. We played at Morecambe first, in the summer of '88 and he really liked us so we ended up doing Blackpool the following year.

We had an agent in Bolton called Tom Ivers at Cream Entertainment. They're still going to this day I believe.

As well as music I've always been a bit of a petrol head and, as I said, in late 1983 I rented a unit, with another guy, in Claremont Rd in Southport and started messing with cars. We did bodywork and mechanics and made a living - just about. I was playing at night and fixing cars during the day. It used to be a garage and was changed into units by none other than Tony Tenser. So, here I was, 20 years on, involved with Tony again. He'd married a Southport girl and stayed in the town. He had a couple of kids and one of them, Barnaby, still comes to the garage I now own. Sadly, Tony passed away in around 2014/15.

Then I got a call from Calle. Tjaerborg Holidays had been in touch with him looking for entertainers. He asked us if we wanted to go to Lanzarote to play at La Santa Sport, a very upmarket holiday resort. There were a couple of people, Karen Lamb and Kim Tell, absolutely great guys, who were running the entertainment there and they'd offered us a fabulous deal. The actual manager was called Kenneth, but he left the running of the entertainment to Karen and Kim. We jumped at it.

And it was a bloody good gig. We would fly out on the Thursday and play on the Saturday night for an hour or one hour fifteen and that was it. We would then fly home the following Thursday. We didn't get any money as such but we got a week's free holiday, full board, for two people We did that about three times a year for four years. Super, super gig for the loveliest people. I'm still in touch with Karen, Kim and Kenneth today.

We each got two air tickets out there every time we went so we could take someone if we wanted. In those days it didn't matter whose name was on the ticket or if the person at check-in matched up with the person on the ticket. There wasn't that level of security back then.

If I'm being really honest now, I took a lady friend with me the first couple of times we went but we often used to sell the spare tickets. You could get £150 for them though we did give them away to friends sometimes. Ann and the kids came out one time when Terry took his family out.

Again, they wanted a four-piece so we got in touch with Phil Barrett, who was still in Denmark, and he made up the fourth member of the band. He and his wife used to fly from Denmark, to Lanzarote, on the Tuesday and the rest of us flew from Manchester Airport on the Thursday.

The first time we went there, Phil was waiting for us at the club when we got off the airport bus.

'Trust me, guys,' he says, 'this place is not for us.'

At this time we were four overweight guys in our thirties and this was a very upmarket sports club. Daly Thomson trained there; Millwall Football Team were there once when we were; Linford Christy and Tessa Sanderson trained there. People paid serious money to use this place.

They had an Olympic sized pool which we actually got thrown out of one time because we were fooling around, chucking each other in, and generally messing about like kids. They said it was for the serious swimmers – cheeky sods!

In December 1986 I decided it was time to have fingers in other pies and I bought a garage called Walmayne Motors, in Southport, which I still have to this day. It was so named because the guy I bought it off was called Walter and his wife's name was May. I kept the name because it was an established business. Owning the garage also enabled me to go away playing wherever and whenever I wanted because the staff would take over. My third son, David, runs it these days.

Over the next few years Brent, Terry and myself gigged around the local clubs. Bernard had left Barratts by now and had got a job as entertainments manager at The Hindley Social Club in Hindley Green, Wigan. He worked there for some years and, in that time, he booked us on several occasions and more often than not he ended up playing the last spot with us.

In June 1990 Bernard decided to leave the club and re-join us properly. We'd got a week's gig in Denmark and we sailed the next day.

Our roadie at the time, Ian Baker, has a favourite story from this particular trip. I had two front teeth on a metal plate which were replacing the teeth I'd lost in '66 when I had the crash. One of the teeth detached itself from the plate while we were on the boat, but luckily, I was able to retain it. I procured some superglue from someone and glued the tooth back on. Ian always recalls waking up to a bit of commotion in the cabin which Brent, Ian, Terry and myself were sharing. Terry had had a bit too much to drink and decided he wanted to tie a luggage label round my willy. Ian thought he was having a nightmare when he woke up to see the deed being done. He then looked across and saw my teeth drying on the bedside light. It really freaked him out. We thought he was going to have a heart attack. To this day he loves to tell that story.

We played five gigs over five days during that visit and sailed back to Harwich the following Tuesday. We then went straight to Bournemouth to play for one of the big union conferences on the Thursday. We'd played for them the year before in Blackpool and we must have gone down well because they'd rebooked us for this one and had given us more money. Mind you even this didn't cover the expenses of the travel and accommodation.

It was then Terry's turn to decide he was ready for a change and he left us and we continued on the merry-go-round as a three-piece.

In 1996 I was approached by a guy called Chris Purcell. He lived in Formby at the time and was a budding film director. Channel 4 were allocating 6 programmes to new directors and were asking for ideas. Chris had seen us play and asked if we would be interested in doing one of these slots. He had an idea for a documentary called 'Reflected Glory' which basically followed our career doing The Beatles' stuff. Of course, we said yes.

If I remember rightly, Channel 4 gave him a budget of £25,000. It was produced by a company in Manchester called Barraclough Carey and they had all the contacts for sound and light equipment, cameras etc. The cameraman was a freelance guy called Nick Plowwright, who I believe was at the top of his game and still is. They hired a special camera with a wide lens because they wanted to sell the program to Japan and at the time Japan wanted everything in wide lens.

They spent five days, with us, following us around. They filmed me in my garage and interviewed Bernard in his car. They also interviewed The Bootleg Beatles who, for some reason, seemed to have the market sewn up. They filmed me going to see one of their shows to get my take on it. They even interviewed a couple of our wives.

At the end of the show they filmed us playing at The Kingsway Club. The show was aired on 5th October 1996 on Channel 4 and it's still available to watch on YouTube today.

I ran into Chris Purcell again about 12 years ago. He was working for The Discovery Channel and doing very well.

In the same year I got yet another call from Calle,

'What are you guys up to?' he said. 'Are you still doing The Beatles thing?'

'Just weekends,' I told him, 'but only as a three-piece.'

'Well there's been a huge upsurge of interest, in Denmark, in The Beatles' Anthology. There's been a lot of Beatles footage of it on TV over here,' he said.

He says, 'Why don't you come back and play over here? I can put a lot of work your way, but you'll need to be a four-piece to do The Beatles.'

So, once again back on the merry-go-round. Now Terry had ended up joining another band but I happened to know that they'd recently split so I contacted him and he agreed to do the Danish gigs with us. I was really pleased because as we'd all played together before it was much easier to take Terry as opposed to anyone else who we'd have to train up. Terry suggested he come to a couple of gigs in England and play along with us to get back into it. He also appeared with us in 'Reflected Glory'.

The first gig with him was actually Ian Baker's future wife, Beryl's 50th birthday party. We also had a gig the next day, which was the Sunday, at the synagogue in Portland Street, Southport. Most Jewish gigs were on a Sunday because of Saturday being their Sabbath.

We played the first set of Beryl's party and then my phone started to ring. It was the guy who ran the entertainment at the synagogue wanting to know where we were. I told him the gig was the next night.

'It's not,' he said. 'There are 200 people waiting to hear you play.' He informed me that the Sabbath had finished at sunset. Apparently, it ran from sunset on the Friday to sunset on the Saturday. Being February, it had, of course, gone dark at about 5pm. I felt dreadful and had to explain to Beryl that we had to go but she was brilliant about it. All the guys in the club helped us move the gear in double quick time and we went to the synagogue albeit an hour and a half late. We still played the allotted time they'd booked us for but it took me a while to claw back the full fee, lol.

We started going over to Denmark about once a month, then twice a month and before long we were going every week. We were still really popular and eventually we started doing 10-day stints. Again, this was a bit too much for Terry and again he left us.

Then it was Calle's turn to have a great idea. There was a singer, called Ib Grønbech who was very big at the time in Denmark and had had a mega hit with a song he wrote himself. It was a strange translation into English. Something like Mother, Why Can't I have my Hair like the Beatles? His group had just disbanded, and Calle thought it would be a great idea for us to work with him.

Ib sent us about a dozen songs to listen to but again he wanted a four-piece. This time we managed to get a friend of Bernard's, called Alan Watkinson (Wokkey), to take Terry's place. He started coming with us over to Denmark at the weekends. We did Thursday Friday, Saturday and got very well paid for it so he was happy to do that for a while. Then he also decided it was too much and we lost him too.

Next we got a Danish guy called Benny Bach. Benny owned a Danish record company which was very successful in fact Ib recorded with them. He started playing keyboard with us on the side. We did a lot with Grønbech including his TV cabaret shows; and we were very much part of the show. He used to have us dressed as miners and we would walk on from the back in overalls and miners' hats with lights. It was a great success.

On those shows we were known as The Liverpool Quartet and we would do little sketches on our own. For example, Ib taught me how to say, 'Do you live alone?' in Danish. I would say it to the ladies and everyone thought it was hilarious. Bernard was taught to say, 'Have you got any money?' again in Danish, to members of the audience. It was very funny, and they loved it. We regularly played to packed houses, anything from 200-800 people which was a lot in Denmark.

We also did what they called a review show with him 3 nights a week, at a local restaurant. It was basically an old-fashioned variety show. We did 2 sets, each lasting about fifty minutes.

The review shows were extremely Danish in every sense and it was the first time ever that an English band had performed in one. It was unheard of generally but for some reason we went down very well. Ib had us doing a variety of things onstage. For example, I played the ukulele and sang 'Have a Drink on Me'. The audience thought it was great.

But all of this takes its toll on family life and Brent left us Christmas '98 because of family commitments. His little boy, Louis had just started school and he wanted to be at home.

Maybe I should have done a bit more of that kind of stuff but I didn't, and Ann and I had split up the year before. She got fed up with the lifestyle we were leading and being on her own a lot.

In fairness, I have to admit, I could have tried a lot harder. For example, unless we had to play for Ib on a Sunday afternoon Brent used to get the first flight home from Jutland, to Copenhagen at 06:30 on a Sunday morning and then fly on to Manchester. He'd be in Manchester by 10 and home for 11. Bernard and I didn't want to get up at such an early hour, so we got the later flight at 17:30. That obviously didn't go down too well with the Mrs and there was a lot of other stuff too.

As much as I knew I'd asked for it when she said she didn't want to be married anymore it totally floored me. The house was in her name and so she sold it. It took me about four years to get over the breakup.

In 1999 we had a succession of bass players. We had one guy called Dave. He did most of the first season, but the problem was that Dave had a full-time job in England. He used to take the Thursday off work, come out with us to Denmark, do the reviews and go back home on the Sunday to go back to work on the Monday. This went on for some time until his bosses got fed up with him taking all this time off and he too had to leave us.

We then had a different bass player nearly every week. Ib Grønbech was going nuts but they all knew what they were doing so we couldn't really see why there was a problem. They were all good.

Finally, in the autumn of that year, Wally came back. To be bluntly honest I was dead against it because I didn't think he would stick the long stints away. But thankfully he did and he was great. I have never been so happy to be proved wrong.

The next person to leave was Benny because it was becoming too much for him. We were doing a lot of gigs, all over Denmark, plus TV, and he was the director of his own recording company and had meetings every day. He just couldn't keep up.

To replace him we then got the guy who stayed with us for years until he passed away in 2012. He was called Torben Dahl but we used to call him Benny. It just sounded a bit more English. He was a keyboard player/guitarist.

Ib had once had a big hit with a guy called Jodle Birge. It was a funny song and, the best I can translate it, was called 'Peter's in the Tent and Ole's in the Caravan'. Bernard and I used to do this song in the shows. We used to mime it. Bernard would take off Jodle Birge and of course I was Ib Grønbech. Now, Ib was about six feet two, thin with glasses. I'm about five feet four and not exactly sylphlike so I stood on a beer crate to make myself taller. Bernard dressed up as Jodle Birge in the Alpine hat and pipe. In the music video that went with the track, Ib wore a dressing gown. I also had on a dressing gown but underneath I was wearing a G-string and stockings and suspenders. Near the end of the song I ripped the dressing gown off and the place would be in uproar, especially the women. Then I used to step down off the crate. It always went down really well. It was very, very funny.

In 2001 I decided to take The Beatles thing a little bit further and I put it to Calle. I would go around Liverpool and take photos of places mentioned in their songs; places like Penny Lane for example and put them on slides. I'd go on stage first for about ten to fifteen minutes and explain how Lennon and McCartney met at St Peter's Church, Woolton. I'd could embellish it a bit and tell all about Penny Lane and the shelter in the middle of the roundabout, the places they played, such as The Cavern and what it was like in the early days. I wanted to call it 'The Beatles' Story'. Calle loved it but wanted to have us in proper suits again. To keep costs down I suggested that we just got the jackets and wore black pants. That was fine but Calle insisted on the collarless jackets. Funnily enough The Beatles didn't actually wear those jackets for very long but somehow, they define them. We found a very good seamstress called Jette who made them up for us.

The line-up was Torben (Benny), Bernard, Terry (Wally) and me. Benny had a great job at the time. He was an accountant for a large electricity company and his boss was a musician. It basically meant he could do what he wanted where we were concerned which was great because we had 10-day tours of Sweden and Norway lined up. He would take the time off and often take his own car and I paid for the juice.

We played with Grønbech for 3 or 4 years and we did The Beatles' Story concerts at the same time. I think the biggest Beatles' Story tour we did was in 2002 when we had 44 dates.

It took off beyond our wildest dreams and gradually we went our own way. We did the occasional gig with Ib but not much. It was a lot more than just a tribute show and we were overwhelmed by the number of gigs we got and the general interest from other Scandinvian countries, especially The Faroe Islands and Greenland. The gigs were always packed out. Every single night.

In 2003 I went to live in Denmark. I bought an old farm with outbuildings which was great for me for messing around with my old cars. Wally and Bernard used to commute from England.

I also started to do other work for Calle acting as

tour manager for a lot of artists he brought over such as The Searchers, Johnny Logan, The Bellamy Brothers and Billy Swan.

One artist he brought over was Linda Gail Lewis, Jerry Lee Lewis's younger sister. The first time I saw her was in a little club in Randers, Denmark. She was fabulous but her backing group were certainly not up to the job. The bass player seemed to be playing another song half the time and the lead singer contributed pretty much nothing. They said they only liked playing Memphis style roots music. Worse still their general attitude towards her seemed to indicate that they thought they were doing her a favour.

The next day I went into the office. Now Calle was the brother I never had so I always felt I could say what I wanted to him.

I said, 'What the fuck are you doing having those guys backing her?'

Linda was such an easy-going person and wouldn't complain. But this was a lady who toured the world with her brother to packed arenas and theatres. A lot of artists would not have done another gig with these idiots. Unfortunately, Calle had his agent's hat on and said he couldn't afford to pay a band top money on top of Linda's fee and expenses.

Then he asked me to go and see another show with him that night as he wanted my opinion; so, I went with him. The band consisted of two girl singers, a keyboard player, a bass guitarist, a rhythm guitarist and a lead singer. They played '50s and '60s style rock 'n roll and they were extremely good.

On the way home Calle says, 'I think I'll book them for a ten-day tour next year.'

When I got home I started to think about all this and thought *Why don't we put our own show together?* We knew enough great musicians who would be a lot less expensive because they wouldn't need flight tickets, hotels, expenses etc. These things could cost more than the actual wages sometimes. I also thought of Linda.

We were running The Beatles' Story down a bit. The success of it had been astonishing but Denmark is a small country and we knew it was best to not over expose it.

Calle thought it was a great idea but reminded me that The Bootles wouldn't be able to back Linda and of course he was right. I contacted her first with the idea and she was really up for it. I then contacted a guitarist/keyboard player who had worked with us on the second Beatles' Story tour in place of Benny (Torban) who hadn't been able to get time off work for that particular tour. He'd actually worked with Linda before. He also said he could get us two girl singers and a sax player. I asked Calle if we could ask Bernard to play bass and sing and he agreed to that so we were ready to rock.

I sat down and started getting a show together. The majority of gigs would be in small theatres and art centres with seated audiences. I worked on putting a theme together to make the shows flow. I called the show *'Rock Roll & Remember'*.

Morten had a recording studio and we started rehearsing there and after two or three four-hour sessions we had a great show to put on the road.

The band (Morten Kjeldson (guitar/keyboard), Niels Matieson (sax), Bernard Southern (bass) and yours truly on drums) would start off with an instrumental. We had two girls in the show, Trine Rebold and Christina Bianca, who would then come on and do a song each. Then after about five numbers Linda would come on and we'd all fill the spot up for 45 minutes playing old classics that everyone knew. After a half hour break we, the band, would open the second set. We'd play one number and then I would bring Linda on and we'd all be on stage again. She was amazing. She always gave 120% doing rock 'n roll standards and of course her brother's hits. It was a truly fabulous show even if I say so myself. We had over three great years with Linda doing 15 day tours each year. We also brought out a 12 track CD and a live DVD; and we appeared in numerous TV shows in Scandinavia.

And this was how it was until a terrible thing happened. During my time in Denmark I always went back to England for Christmas. My parents were getting on, so I'd spend it with them. Then I'd go back to Denmark for New Year. We'd usually have a gig on New Year's Eve anyway.

On 22 December 2007, at around 8pm, I was at my dad's in Southport (my mother had died in the February of that year) when the phone rang. It was a guy called Per Kastrup, who rented an apartment to the guys when they came over. He told me to phone Thomas, Calle's business partner, because he'd heard that Calle had died. I rang him straight away and he confirmed that it was true. He'd had a massive stroke. It was a great shock. I was devastated. Later that night Calle's daughter, Christine, also rang to tell me but of course I told her I already knew.

She was quite relieved because she had loads of people to ring. Calle was a popular guy and I think their reactions to the news was getting to her a bit. She got back to me a few days later however to ask me to be a pallbearer with 3 of his sons and two friends and of course I was honoured. Johnny Logan sang Danny Boy to a packed church. A lot of Danish stars were there plus Barry and Geoff from Herman's Hermits as well as Phil from Sailor.

His funeral was on 2nd January. I flew to Denmark for the funeral on New Year's Day and travelled back to England on the 3rd as I was going on holiday to Malta.

I was on a tour bus in Malta when my phone rings. It was Thomas phoning from Denmark. 'Menzies,' he says, 'you need to come into the office as soon as you get back. We've got mega problems and you know more about the English side of things than anyone else.'

After I got back from Malta I had a meeting with Thomas, Christine and Torben, who worked in the office as a booking agent. They explained that I had more knowledge of the English bands than they did and they'd got into a bit of a mess. The problem was that Calle didn't keep any documents; everything was in his head. For example, he'd book a band for 4 nights for a certain fee then he'd ring them up asking if they could do 2 more nights but none of it was logged.

One of the big 70s English bands was booked to play at a festival. On Calle's computer there was an email confirming the gig. After I'd been there a couple of weeks I started ringing people to make sure all was in order and the leader of this band said this gig was never confirmed and they'd taken another booking in Spain. He changed his tune when I forwarded that e-mail to him, but he still insisted on not doing the gig. I said that if the festival wouldn't agree to another band I'd sue him. Luckily, they did but we never used them again.

I went into the office 3 days a week and I managed to sort a lot out. The first thing I did was sign and send off a contract for £10k that had been hanging around for weeks. I made a phone call to one of the English bands who had never been contacted and sorted the fees out with them. I saved the agency a lot of money all told.

I spent around five months there, until it was sold. During that time, I booked several big names including Dr Hook, The Searchers, The Tremeloes, Herman's Hermits, Jonny Logan, The Rubettes and many more. I organised travel and accommodation and negotiated the fees.

I was still playing with the band but after Calle's death things started to run down. We stayed there another couple of years but in August 2010 we finally packed up and came back to England.

We still continued to go back to Denmark for special functions including, in 2012, a big 60s fest in Holstebro. There was a club which was fondly known as The Wednesday club. It was in a park. They had functions throughout the year but the big 60s fest was in August. It was a huge event. It was also the last gig Torben (Benny) ever did for us. He too died the following January. They ran six Wednesday nights through the summer and we played there with The Tremeloes and The Rubettes.

In the July of 2013 we also played at a big 70th birthday party for a lady called Karen Salling who owned department stores throughout Denmark. She got to know us through Peter Singaard an arts centre manager who had booked us many times before. She knew absolutely everyone, and we played there with a lot of big Danish names; Jasper Lundgaard being but one. It was like the who's who of Danish entertainment. A good friend of ours, Chimbo, stood in for Torben. He had, and still has, a band called Chimbo's Revival. Chimbo himself is a great singer, keyboard player and guitarist.

We didn't know it but it would be the last time we would play in Denmark.

From then on, we became pretty much semi-retired. The line-up changed again and became Brent, Bernard and myself. Then George re-joined us a couple of years later when he'd ended up back in the area. For some reason we'd retained our popularity and got some very good gigs, but we were all getting older and a couple of the band members weren't in the best of health. Brent in particular had heart and chest problems.

We had a friend called Phil Collins who was a local businessman. In the summer of '15 we were scheduled to play at his wife's 60th birthday party. I got a call about 10 days before the event from Brent's son, Darryl, to say his dad was in hospital and in Intensive Care. They said that his oxygen sats were so low that he was unlikely to survive. Being the trooper that he was he pulled through but I ended up doing the party with a Searchers' tribute band from Liverpool and we got the job done.

The next day I did a gig for another businessman with Bernard and Terry, our old bass player, and we then took some time off until Lightbulb was well enough to re-join us. But to be honest, he never really did regain his health and often struggled to play.

Brent had been a member of The Bootles from the outset and, as I said, we were all getting older. I decided that, when he couldn't go on any more, we would disband for good.

That end came in March 2016 when we again played at a private birthday party. Brent struggled from the word go. It was upstairs for a start which was a major challenge for his breathing. He sat to play and at the end of the evening people started shouting for more. Brent turned to me and said, 'Al, I can't play another note.'

Later he took me to one side and quietly told me that he thought it was time we found someone else to replace him.

I had never had any intention to do that and so, true to my word, that night became The Bootles' final gig.

*It was with great sadness that, shortly before this paperback went into publication, we had to add Brent to the In Memory Of page. He passed away peacefully on 5th November 2019.

Left to right back: Alan Watkinson, Bernard Southern Front: Brent Pickthall, Alan Menzies. Courtesy of Walter Brown

Left to right: Alan Menzies, Terry Walters, Brent Pickthall ,
Courtesy of Walter Brown

Left to right: Niels Mathiasen, Morten Kjeldson, Alan Menzies, Bernard Southern

NoName the Band

For about a year before the disbanding of The Bootles I had also played on a Thursday night at the Lathom, in Seaforth, with a band called The Dominoes. George was playing there with them and I started playing when their drummer Peter (Mesh) Stephenson passed away. I played with a few other bands there as well.

In the summer of 2015, I was standing in for a drummer with one of these groups at The Lankycats, in Standish. Steve White and Derek Boak were playing in a band called Equal Terms on the same night. We were last on.

When we'd finished Derek came up and said, 'You really kept that together'.

At the time their band had two drummers. One worked in London so could only do weekends and the other needed a lot of notice to play because of his job. I'd seen them play a few times and had been particularly impressed by Derek's singing and how Steve harmonised very well with him.

I said that I didn't want to step on anyone's toes but I had a gig lined up at The Lakeside Café, in Southport, and were they interested in joining me. Because this gig was in the afternoon it meant that if they had an evening commitment they could still do it.

I had a meeting at The George in Southport with Steve, Derek and their lead guitarist, but I knew within 10 minutes that it wasn't going to work with him. He was set in his ways and absolutely refused to play rock and roll.

I rang Steve the next day and told him what I thought. He said, 'Fuckin' Hell it hasn't taken you long to suss that out'.

Steve and Derek were still interested in us getting together so I said, 'I know a good guitarist', and I contacted George Eccles, who was also floating, and the four of us met in Ormskirk.

A couple of weeks later we met again in the Oldy Club, Old Roan, Liverpool. It's the home of the Merseycats, a charity which raises money for various children's charities around Liverpool. This would be around the October time. We put a short set together, maybe 25 minutes and just played standard rock and roll; things we all knew backwards. It was the first time we'd played together though I had of course played with George many times. We really gelled and everyone had a good feeling about it.

By this time, it was too late to do the Lakeside Café gig so we just started rehearsing together. We met up every Monday evening, rehearsing new songs to add to the ones we could all already play. We tried to find things that other bands didn't play. We did popular stuff like The Beatles and The Eagles but not so much the big hits. We tried out lesser known LP tracks and B sides.

The bass player, Steve, is a member of The Freemasons and our first gig was with them the following April. We then did play a gig at The Lake a few weeks later.

On writing this that's 4 years ago and we are still playing together and going from strength to strength. We play two or three times a week, every week, sometimes more. Above all we're still very much enjoying it.

As well as playing regularly with NoName (the Band) I occasionally do '60s weekenders at Butlins and various caravan parks. I usually do these with The Easybeats. On top of that I play with Vince Earl and his band The Attraction a couple of times a year.

You hear a lot of musicians saying that they don't enjoy gigging any more. If I ever feel like that, I'll give up but I can't really see it ever happening.

Over the years I thought we were going to make the big time many times but somehow fame and fortune always managed to elude us. Still, as I look back over my life, do I feel that we made it? You bet!

Alan Menzies. Courtesy of Billy Gill

Left to right: Steve White, Derek Boak, Alan Menzies and
George Eccles.
Courtesy of Billy Gill

Left to right: Steve White, Derek Boak, Alan Menzies and
George Eccles
Courtesy of Billy Gill

Miscellaneous

MARINE VIEW CLUB

KINGSWAY – – SOUTHPORT

THE NEW
TUESDAY TEENAGE CLUB

Presents

THIS WEEK

Tuesday, 10th November, 1964

Southport's No. 1 Group

Rhythm 'n' Blues
Incorporated

PLUS

THE BOYS

YES! TOP GROUPS FOR YOU
EVERY TUESDAY

ADMISSION ONLY - **2/6**

BAR CLOSED   BAR CLOSED

SOFT DRINK BAR OPEN

RHYTHM & BLUES INCORPORATED

From left: Mike McKay, Barry Womersley, Pete Kelly, John
McCaffrey, Alan Menzies
Courtesy of Kin Kelly

Opportunity knocks—in the dark

"Okay, you can practise at the Birkdale Palace Hotel, but you'll have to be out by the time the film company gets back," a local beat group was told recently.

If you would have told these five boys then that before long they would be on their way to London to record the theme tune of a new film, they would never have believed you.

But now the prospect is very much a real one, and on Monday the same five will be recording their own composition, "The Dark," the title song for Tigon Films' latest production.

It all started about a month ago when the five lads—four from Southport and one from Rochdale—decided to get together and form a group under the name of The Jazzmin T.

All having played in groups before, there was John McCaffrey (22), Barry Womersley (23), John Sargen (23), Barry Tweedale (22) and Alan Solomon (20), who, with doubling, play a variety of instruments including piano, organ, flute, sax., oboe bass, guitar and drums.

Then they started practising at the Birkdale Palace Hotel, with the understanding that they would leave when Tigon Films' returned to make their second film at the Hotel.

But when the company arrived they liked the sound The Jazzmin T made and offered them a part playing two numbers in a night club, but the group were destined for even better things.

For together, but mainly from the inspiration of Barry Womersley, they composed "The Dark," which they describe as a "spooky tune with plenty of flute, piano and 12-string guitar." On Monday they are going to London to make the sound track.

The boys consider that they were pretty lucky to get into the film, although separately each has played for a recognised recording label.

Courtesy of The Southport Visiter

Filming of Reflected Glory. Channel 4

A. MENZIES.   Statement for week ended 19th December 1964

                            Balance at 12th December 1964   202 10 1½
      intrigue balance   La Scala Ballroom, Runcorn 12/4/64 (£8 balance)   8   0   0
Sunday, 13th December 1964   Mayson Blues Emily Street, Birmingham   20   0   0
                              Ritz Ballroom, Kings Heath, Birmingham   20   0   0
Monday 14th December 1964   Plaza Ballroom Handsworth, Birmingham   20   0   0
Tuesday 15th December 1964   Wednesbury Youth Centre   25   0   0
Thursday 17th December 1964   Stanley Youth Club, Southport   40   0   0
Friday 18th December 1964   Place Club, Edinburgh, Scotland   25   0   0
Saturday 19th December 1964   Bungy's Club, Edinburgh, Scotland   25   0   0
                                                                                              _____
                                                                                             385 10 1½

Expenses
      Sunday 13th December -   petrol   1 · 2 · 6
                               commission (J. Turner)   3 · 0 · 0
                               petrol   1 · 2 · 0
      Monday 14th December -   petrol   1 · 12 · 0
                               commission (J. Turner)   4 · 0 · 0
                               petrol   1 · 12 · 3
      Tuesday 15th December -   petrol   1 · 7 · 0
                               commission (J. Turner)   5 · 0 · 0
                               petrol   1 · 6 · 0
                               National insurance (W. Hansen)   - · 9 · 5
                               New heater, repairs to heater   34 · 18 · 0
                               repair to bodywork and carburettor }
      Thursday 17th December   commission (J. Turner)   8 · 0 · 0
      Friday 18th December -   petrol   1 · 11 · 9
                               petrol   1 · 12 · 6
                               commission (J. Turner)   5 · 0 · 0
      Saturday 19th December - graduated insurance (W. Hansen)   - · 5 · 1
                               commission (J. Turner)   5 · 0 · 0
                                                                 _____
                                                                                              81 18 9

                                                                                             343 11 4
                  { £8 drawn and paid to each member }   108   0
                  { £8 drawn and paid to road manager }   _____
                                                                                             195 11 4

                            Cash at Halifax Building Society   160   0
                            Cash in hand   23 11
                            Outstanding loan (A. Menzies)   12   0

   Dw.
   20/12/64

NoName the Band, 3rd November 2018, with Linda Barrett, photographer Billy Gill and Kin Kelly
Left to right: Steve White (bass guitar), Billy Gill, Kin Kelly, Linda Barrett, George Eccles (lead guitar), Alan Menzies (drums) and Derek Boak (rhythm guitar)
Courtesy of Billy Gill